HSP Science

Activity Book

Grade K

Visit *The Learning Site!*
www.harcourtschool.com

Printed in the United States of America

ISBN -13: 978-0-15-361078-3
ISBN -10: 0-15-361078-6

16 17 18 19 20 0982 16 15 14

4500478516

Contents

CHAPTER 7 THE WORLD AROUND US

CHAPTER 8 ABOUT ENERGY

CHAPTER 9 ON THE MOVE

Science Safety

Think ahead.

Be neat and clean.

Be careful.

Do not eat or drink things.

Name ______________________________

Science Safety Checklist

_____ I will think ahead.

_____ I will read the directions and follow them.

_____ I will be neat with my materials.

_____ I will take care of all science supplies.

_____ I will clean up when I am done.

_____ I will return all unused materials to my teacher.

_____ I will be careful. I will follow all of the cautions.

_____ I will not taste things I am using in an investigation unless my teacher tells me to.

I can draw a sign I know.

FOLD

Name ______

Our Senses

What does each sign tell us?

Family Note Invite your child to share this book with you. Read the words on each page to your child.

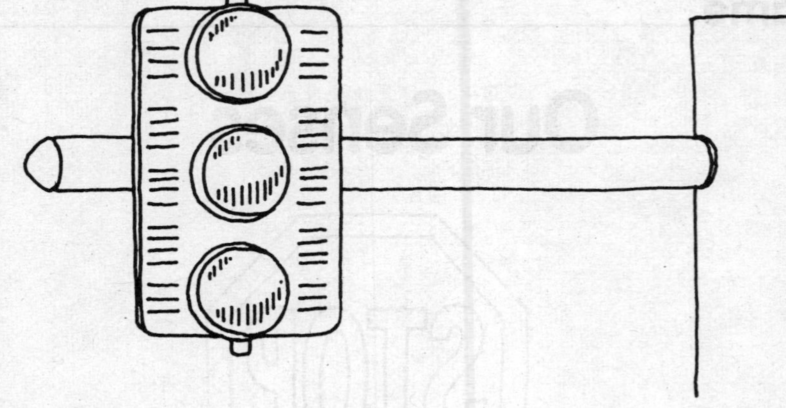

Color this light. Make it say go.

What do you do when you see this?

FOLD

How does this sound?

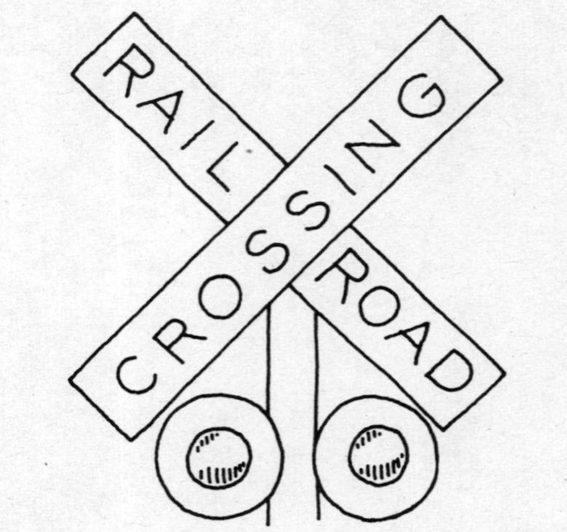

What does this sign tell you?

I can draw an animal with fur.

FOLD

Name ____________________

Animals

Circle the animals that are the same in some way.

Family Note Invite your child to share this book with you. Read the words on each page to your child.

Tell how the chicken changes as it grows.

FOLD

How do these animals move?

I can draw a plant with seeds.

I can draw leaves.

FOLD

Name ______________________

Plants

How are these plants the same?
How are they different?

Family Note Invite your child to share this book with you. Read the words on each page to your child.

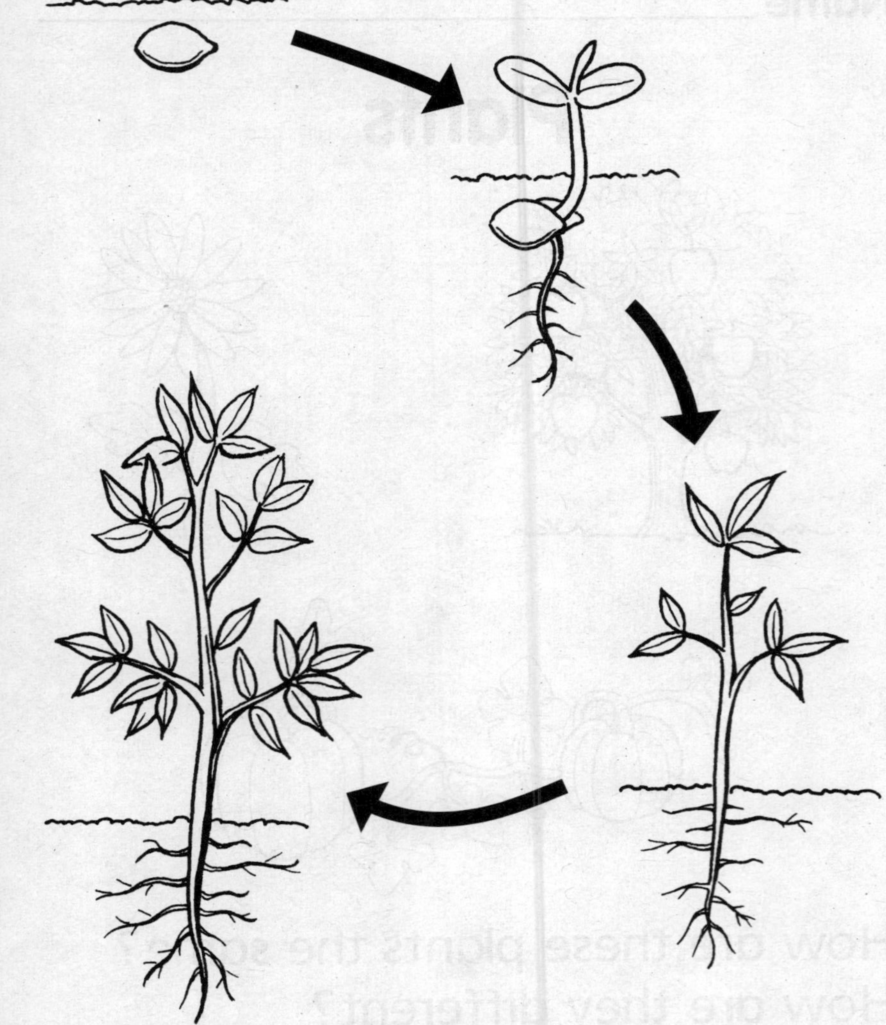

Tell how the plant changes as it grows.

FOLD

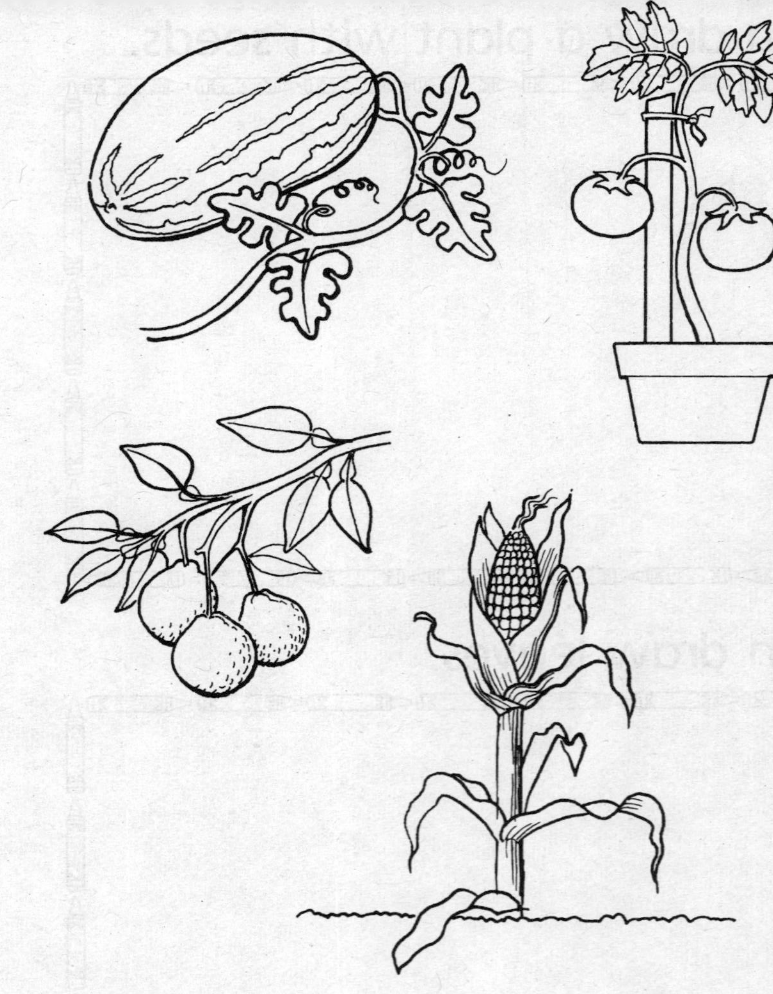

Where are the stems of these plants?

I can show ways to help save animal and plant homes.

FOLD

Name ______________________

Animal and Plant Homes

What do animals need to live?

Family Note Invite your child to share this book with you. Read the words on each page to your child.

How could this harm animal and plant homes?

FOLD

What may happen to the animals and plants that live here?

I can show some ways to care for Earth's land, air, and and water.

FOLD

Name ________________________________

Earth's Land, Air, and Water

I can tell about Earth.

Family Note Invite your child to share this book with you. Read the words on each page to your child.

How does water flow from the top of the mountain to the lake?

FOLD

How has the land been changed?

I can draw a picture to show the weather today.

FOLD

Name ______________________

Weather

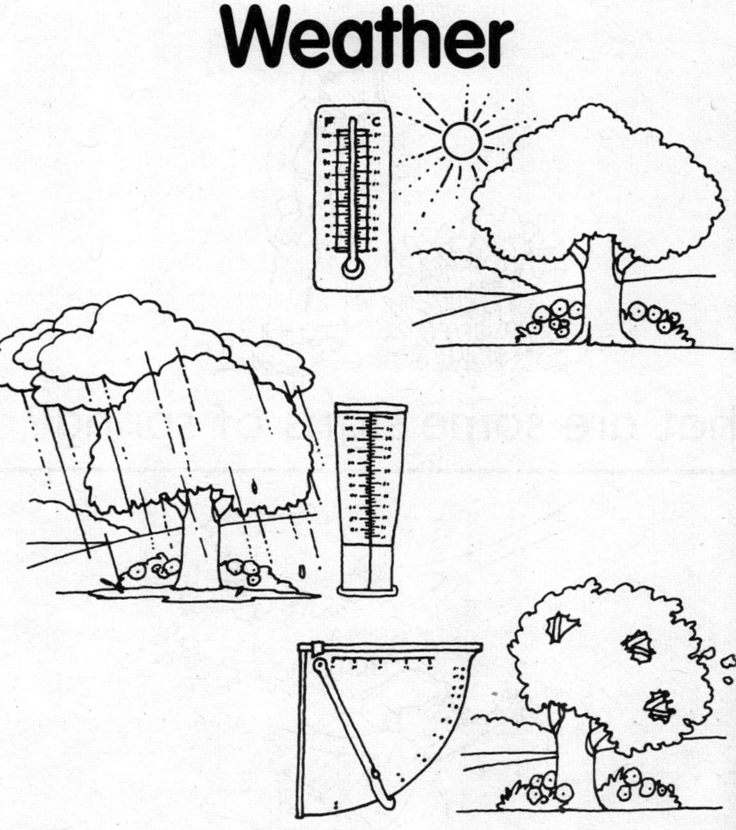

What do these tools tell about the weather?

Family Note Invite your child to share this book with you. Read the words on each page to your child.

What are some signs of spring?

What are some signs of summer?

2

FOLD

What are some signs of fall?

What are some signs of winter?

3

I can draw a day sky.

FOLD

Name ______________________

Day and Night

Color the objects that you might see in the day sky.

Family Note Invite your child to share this book with you. Read the words on each page to your child.

Circle the objects that you might see in the night sky.

FOLD

Draw arrows to show how the sun seems to move.

I can draw a bird above the tree.
I can draw a dog under the tree.

FOLD

Name ______________________

Objects Around Us

Sort these shirts into two groups.
Find another way to sort them.

Family Note Invite your child to share this book with you. Read the words on each page to your child.

Objects can be big and small.
Circle the biggest bear.

FOLD

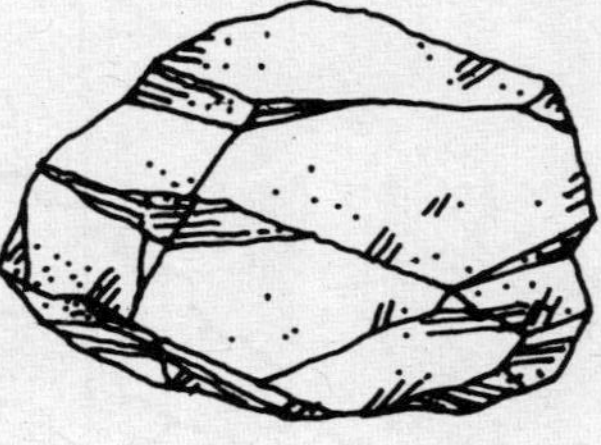

Color the objects that are soft or smooth. Circle the objects that are hard or rough.

FOLD

I can draw a shadow.

4

Name ________________________________

The Sun

Tell how the sun's energy changed the object on the table.

Family Note Invite your child to share this book with you. Read the words on each page to your child.

1

Circle the healthful foods that give you energy.

FOLD

How does the sun's energy make you feel?

I can draw an object I can push.

I can draw an object I can pull.

FOLD

Name ______________________

Motion

Circle the objects that move fast.
Underline objects that move slowly.

Family Note Invite your child to share this book with you. Read the words on each page to your child.

Which objects are being pushed?
Which objects are being pulled?

FOLD

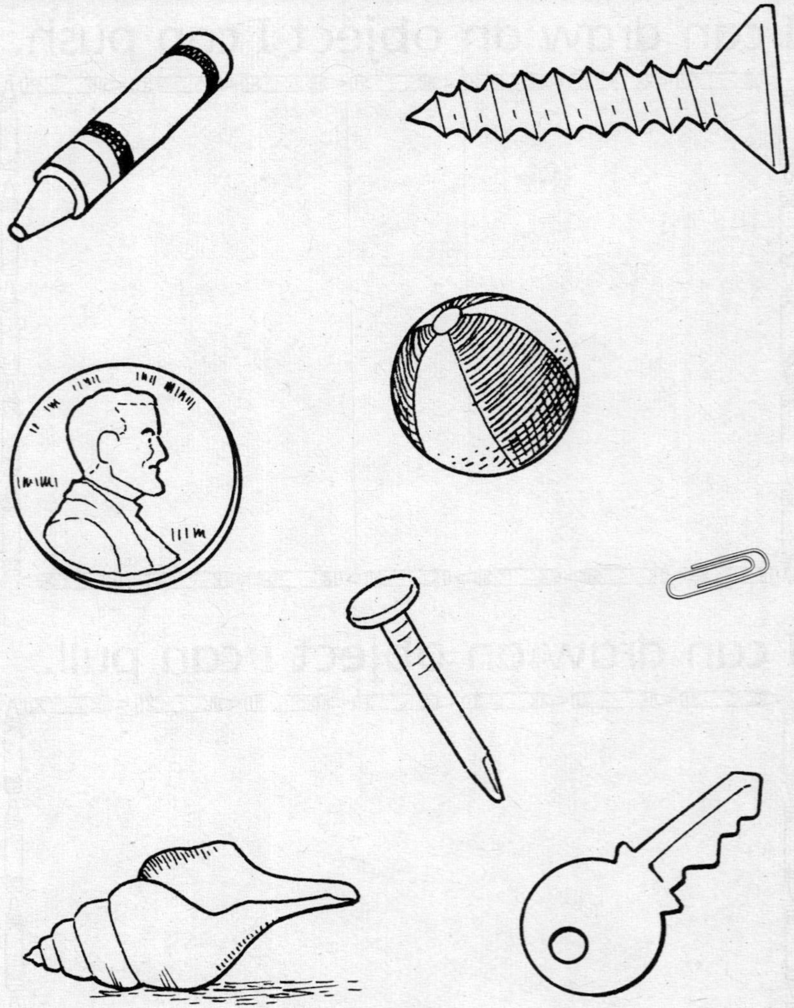

Which objects will a magnet move? How do you know?

Name ____________________

Observe

▲

●

■

▲ Color the picture that shows a child smelling the bread.
● Color the picture that shows a child touching the flower.
■ Color the picture that shows a child looking at the cookie.

Name ______________________

Sort

Circle the children who are comparing objects to learn more.

Name ______________________________

Measure

▲

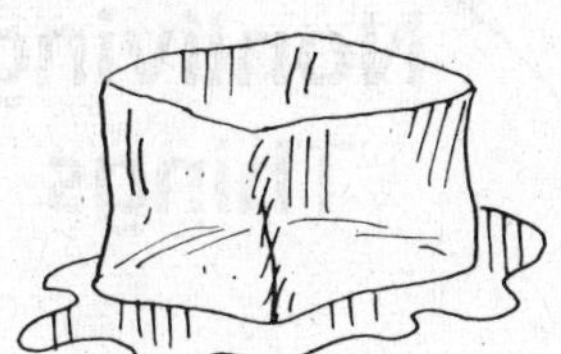

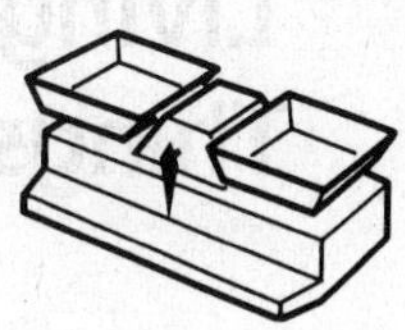

●

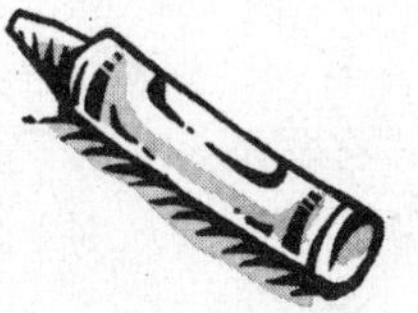

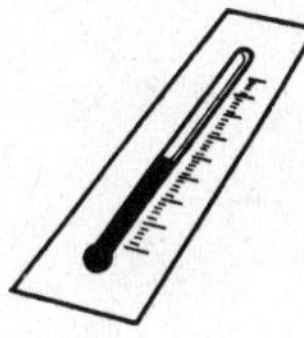

■

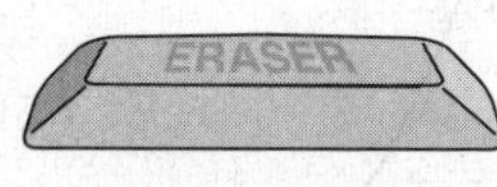

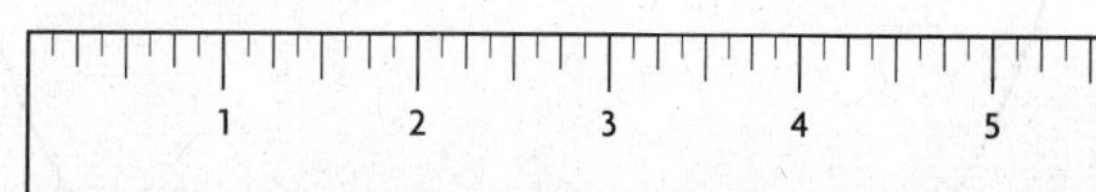

▲ Draw a line to show which tool you would use to measure the temperature.
● Draw a line to show which tool you would use to measure how long something is.
■ Draw two lines to show which tool you would use to measure which weighs more.

Name ____________________

Sort

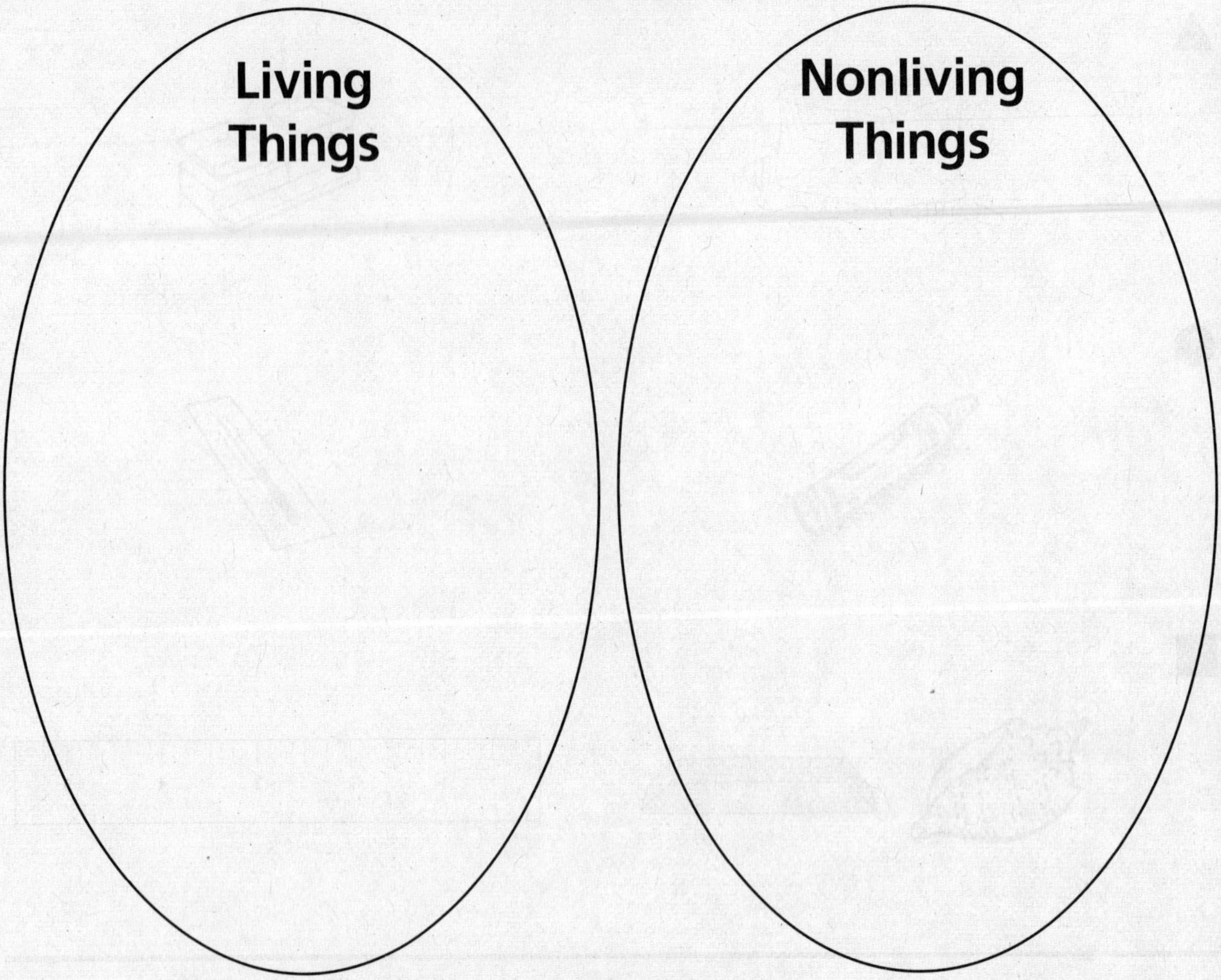

Living Things	Nonliving Things

Cut out the pictures. Sort them into the correct sorting rings. Glue them in place.

Use with pages 12–14.

Name ______________________________

Compare

▲

●

■

▲●■ Color the two animals that are the same in one important way. Draw a line under the animal that is different.

Use with pages 15–17.

Name ______________________

Observe

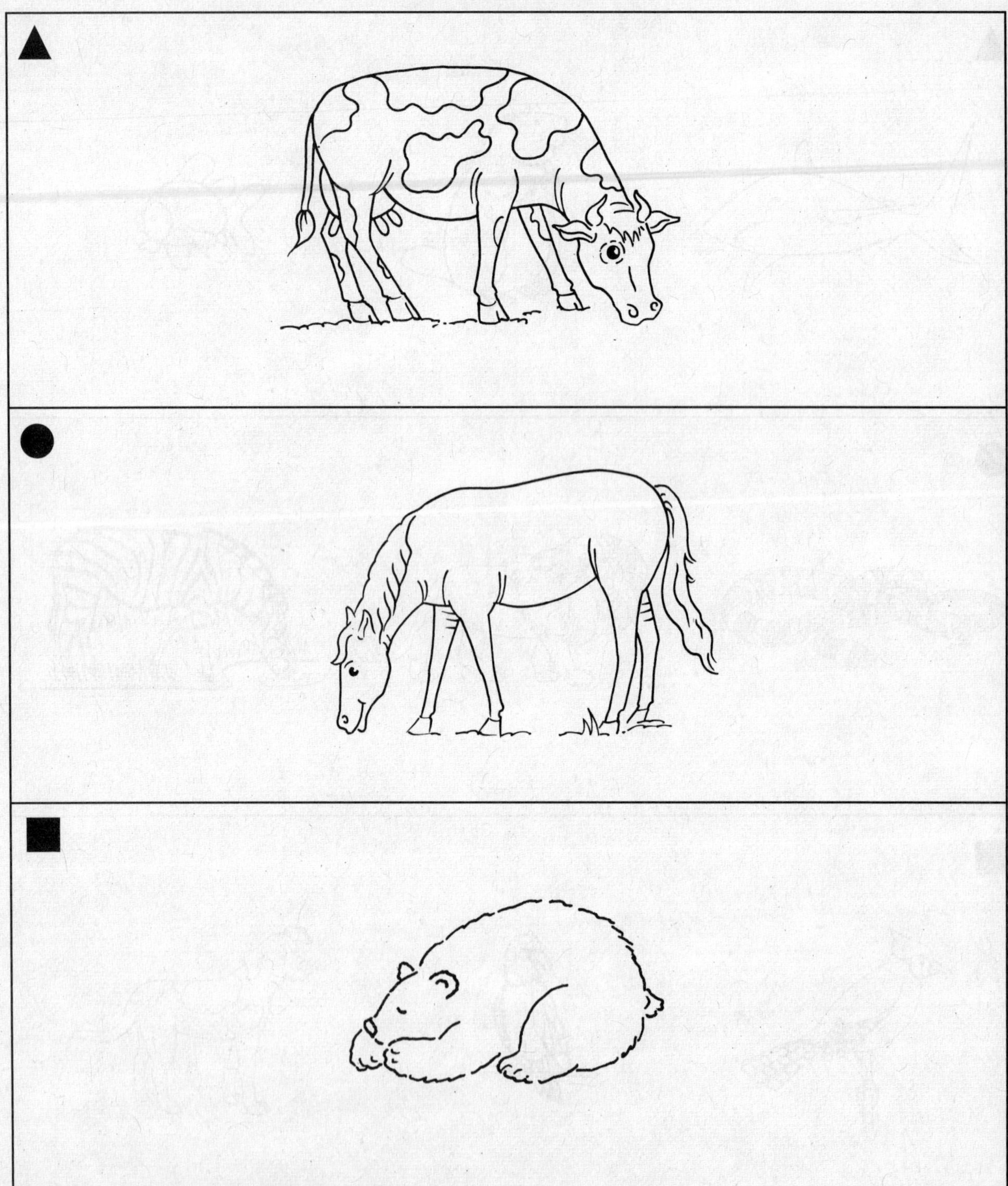

▲ Draw what the cow would eat.
● Draw what the horse would drink.
■ Draw a place for the bear to live.

Use with pages 18–20.

Name ____________________

Sequence

  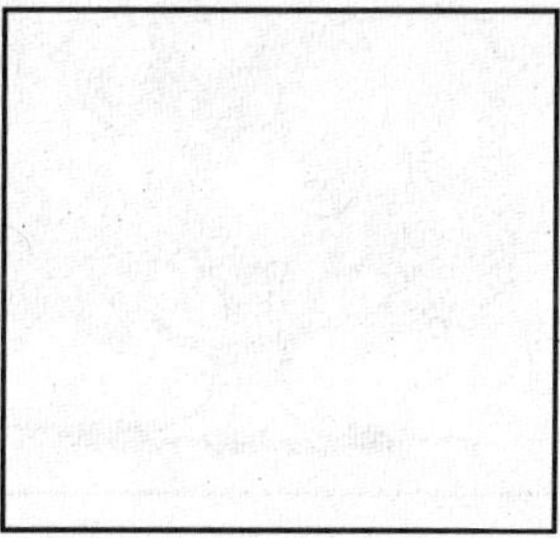  

  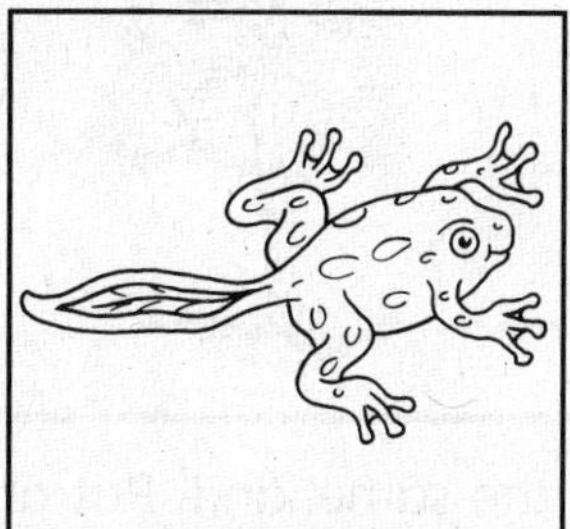  

▲●■ Cut out the pictures below. Glue each picture in the row where it belongs to show what happens first, next, and last.

Use with pages 21–24.

Name ____________________

Draw Conclusions

▲ Shrubs

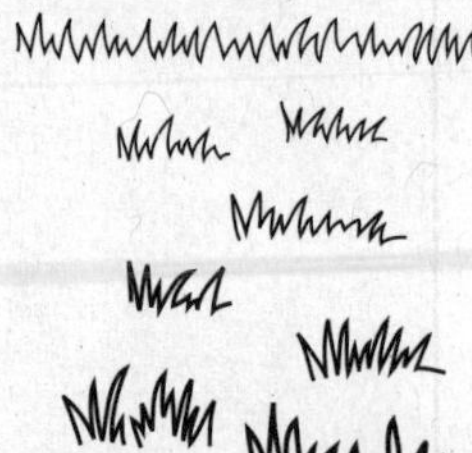

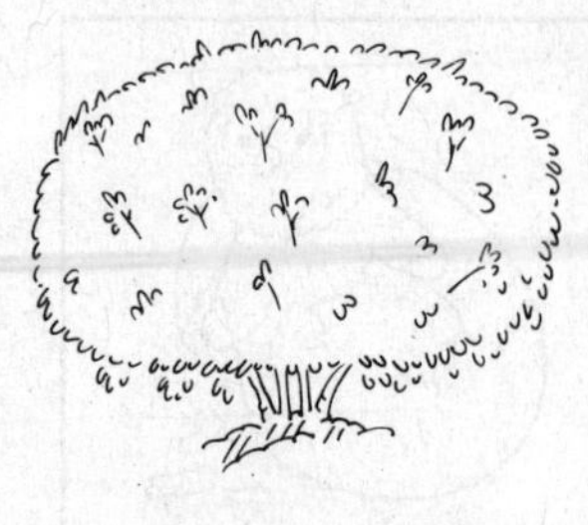

● Trees

■ Grasses

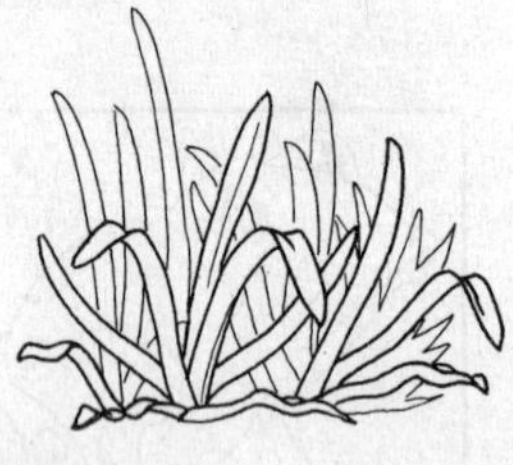
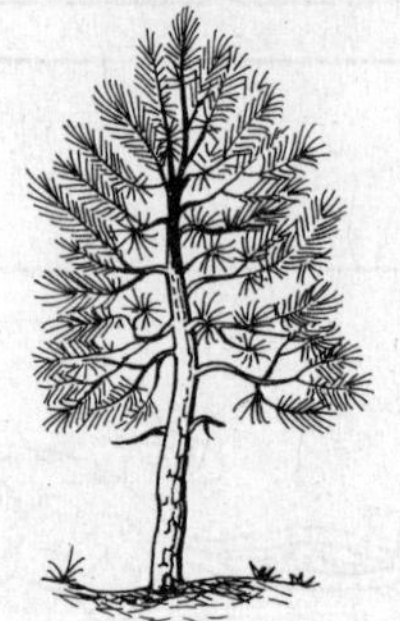

▲●■ Color the two plants that are the same kind. Put an X on the plant that is a different kind.

Name ______________________

Predict

Today ▲

Next Week

Water

Mon.	Tue.	Wed.	Thurs.	Fri.
No	No	No	No	No

●

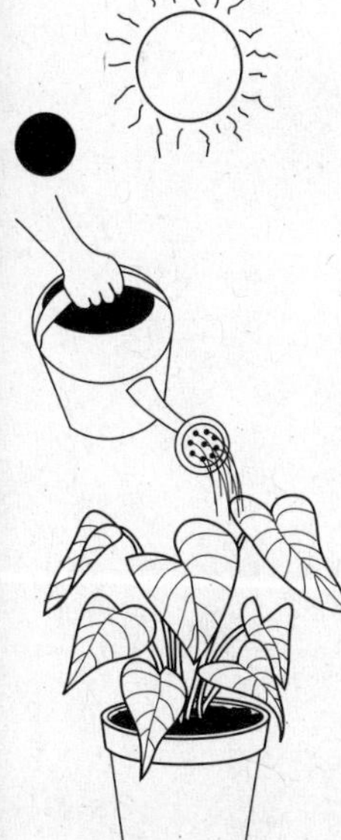

Mon.	Tue.	Wed.	Thurs.	Fri.
Yes	No	Yes	No	Yes

▲● Draw a line to show what you predict will happen to the plant in a week's time.

Name ____________________

Observe

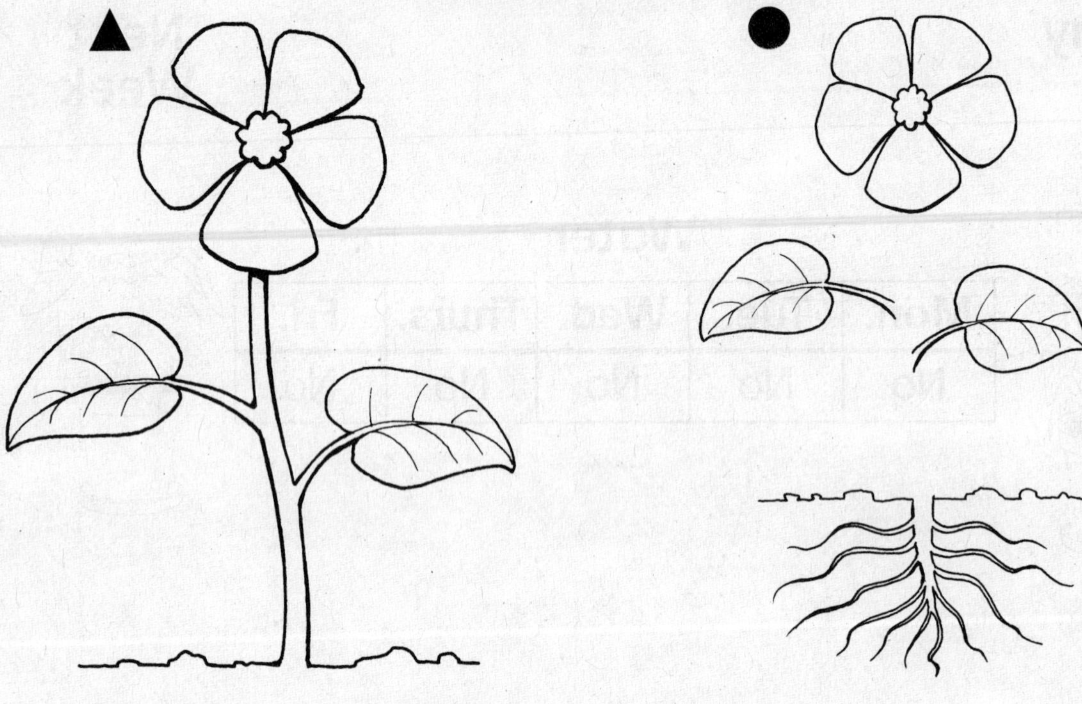

▲ Draw roots for the plant.
● Draw a stem for the plant.
■ Draw leaves for the plant.

Use with pages 32–34.

Name ____________________

Infer

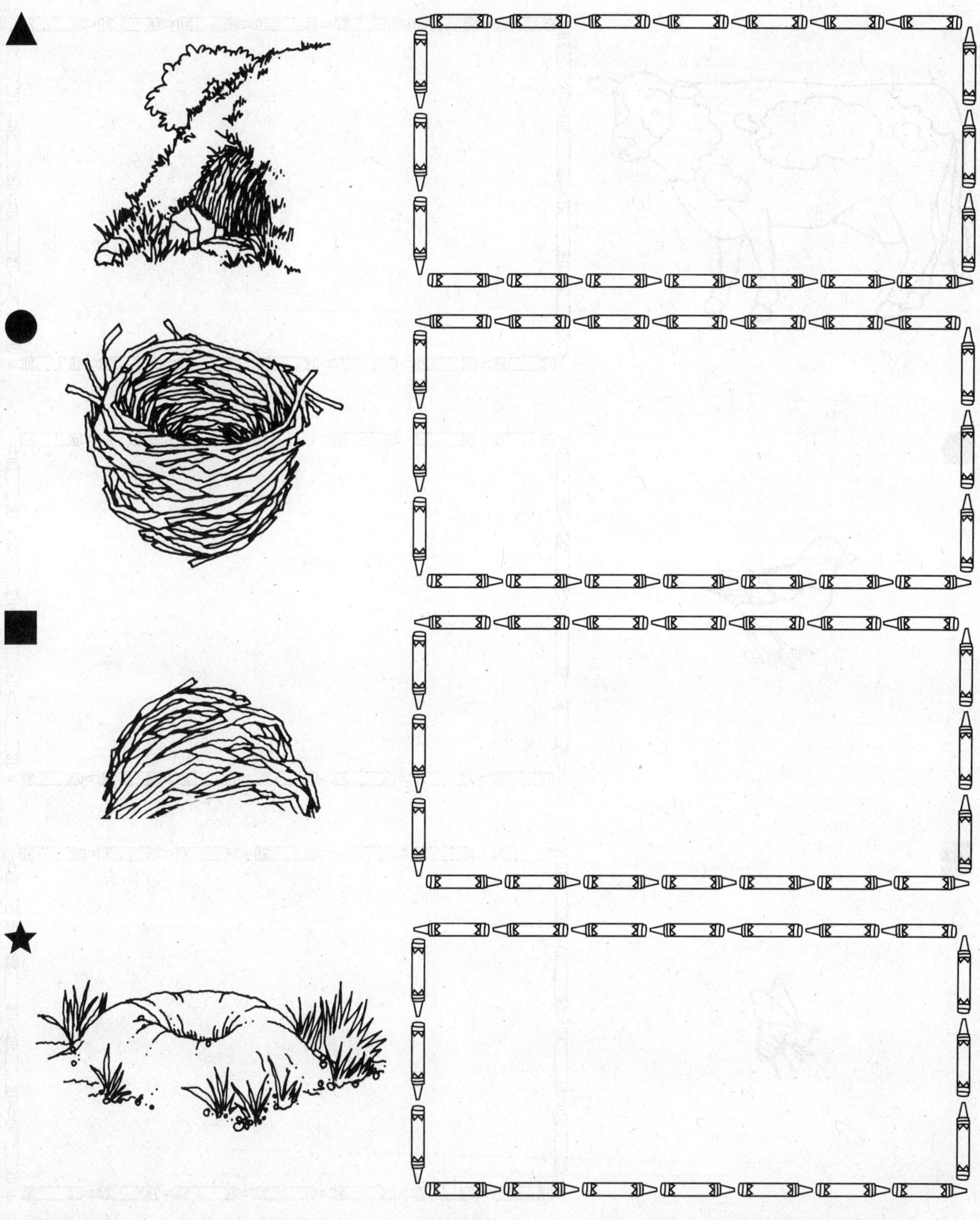

▲●■★ Draw an animal that lives in the home.

Name ________________________________

Communicate

▲●■ Draw a plant or animal that each animal depends on to live.

Name ________________________________

Sort

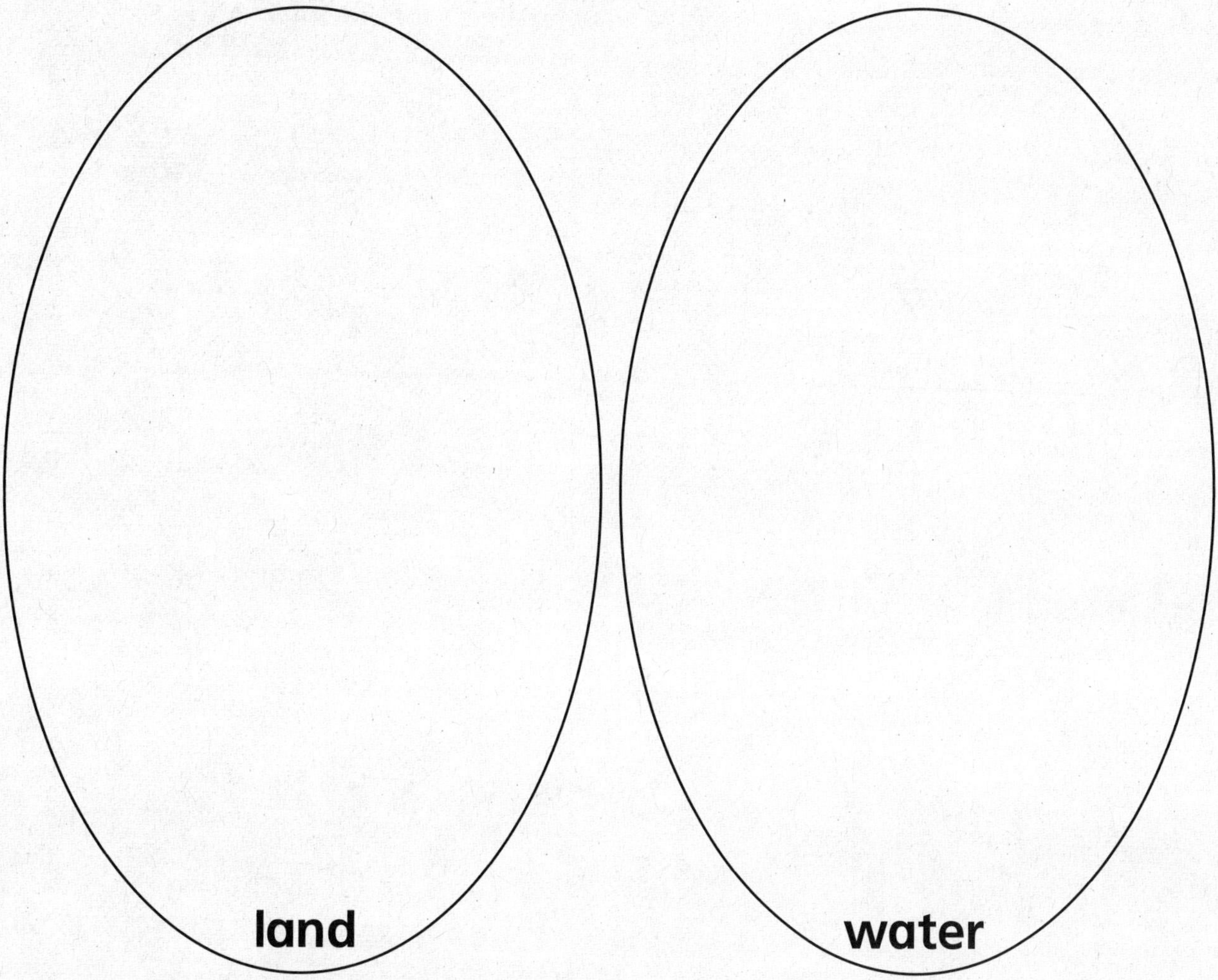

land

water

Cut out the pictures. Glue them where they belong.

Use with pages 47–48.

Name ____________________

Communicate

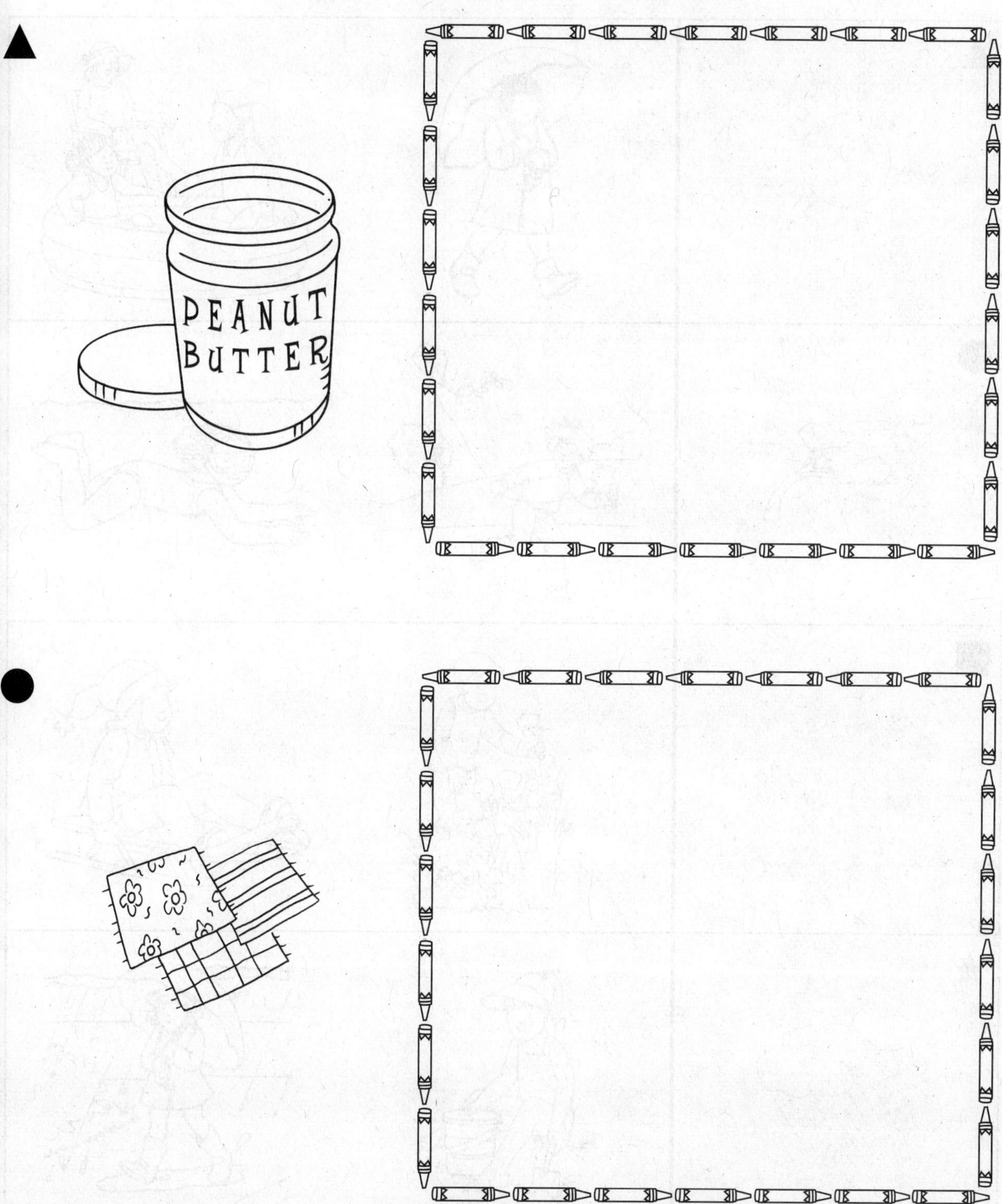

▲● We can help take care of Earth by reusing things such as empty jars and cloth. Draw a picture to show one way you could reuse each material.

Name ______________________________

Observe

▲●■★ Observe the weather symbol. Color the picture that shows what you might do in that kind of weather.

Use with pages 61–63.

Name ____________________

Measure

▲ Look at the first rain gauge. Circle the rain gauge that shows more rain.
● Look at the first rain gauge. Draw the same amount of rain in the other gauge.

Name ________________________________

Sequence

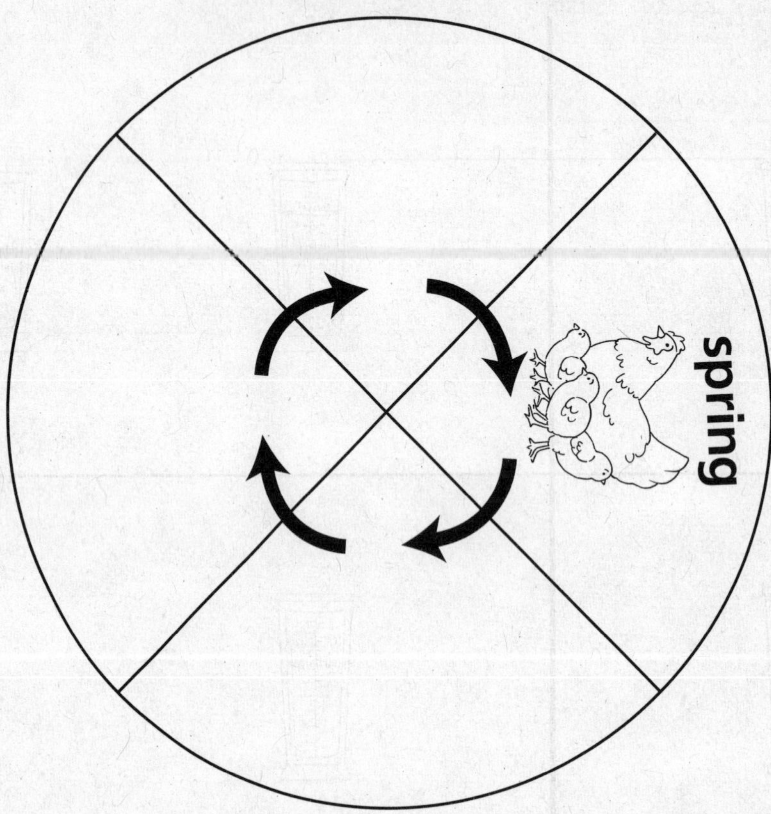

Cut out the pictures of seasons. Glue the pictures on the circle in the correct order to show the sequence of the seasons.

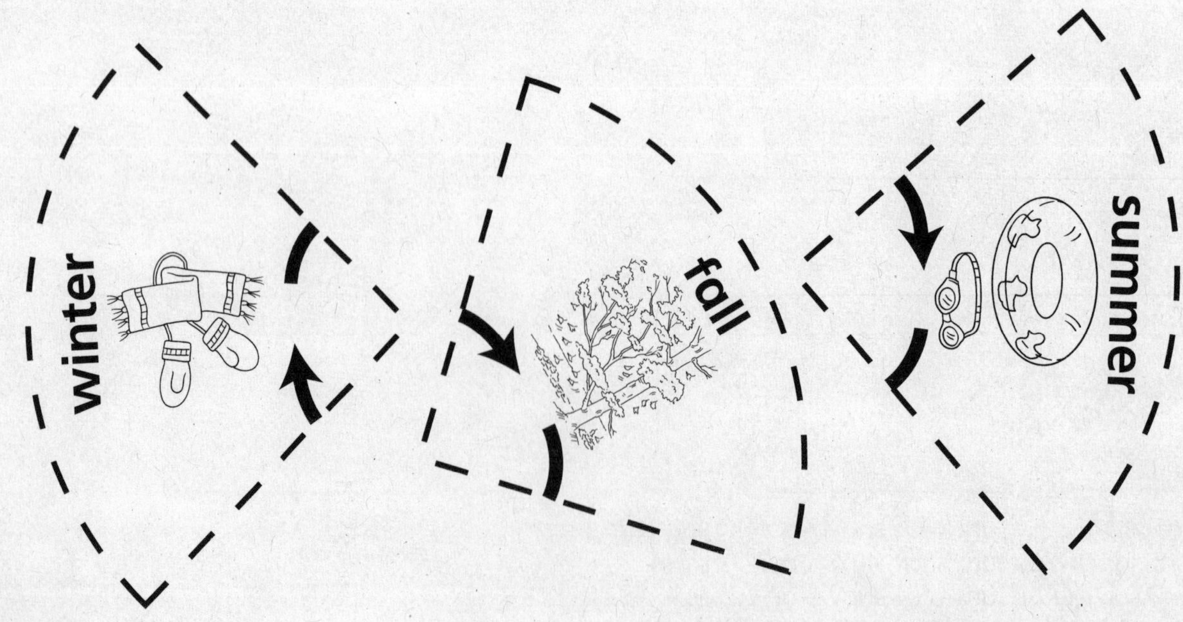

Use with pages 66–71.

Name ______________________________

Observe

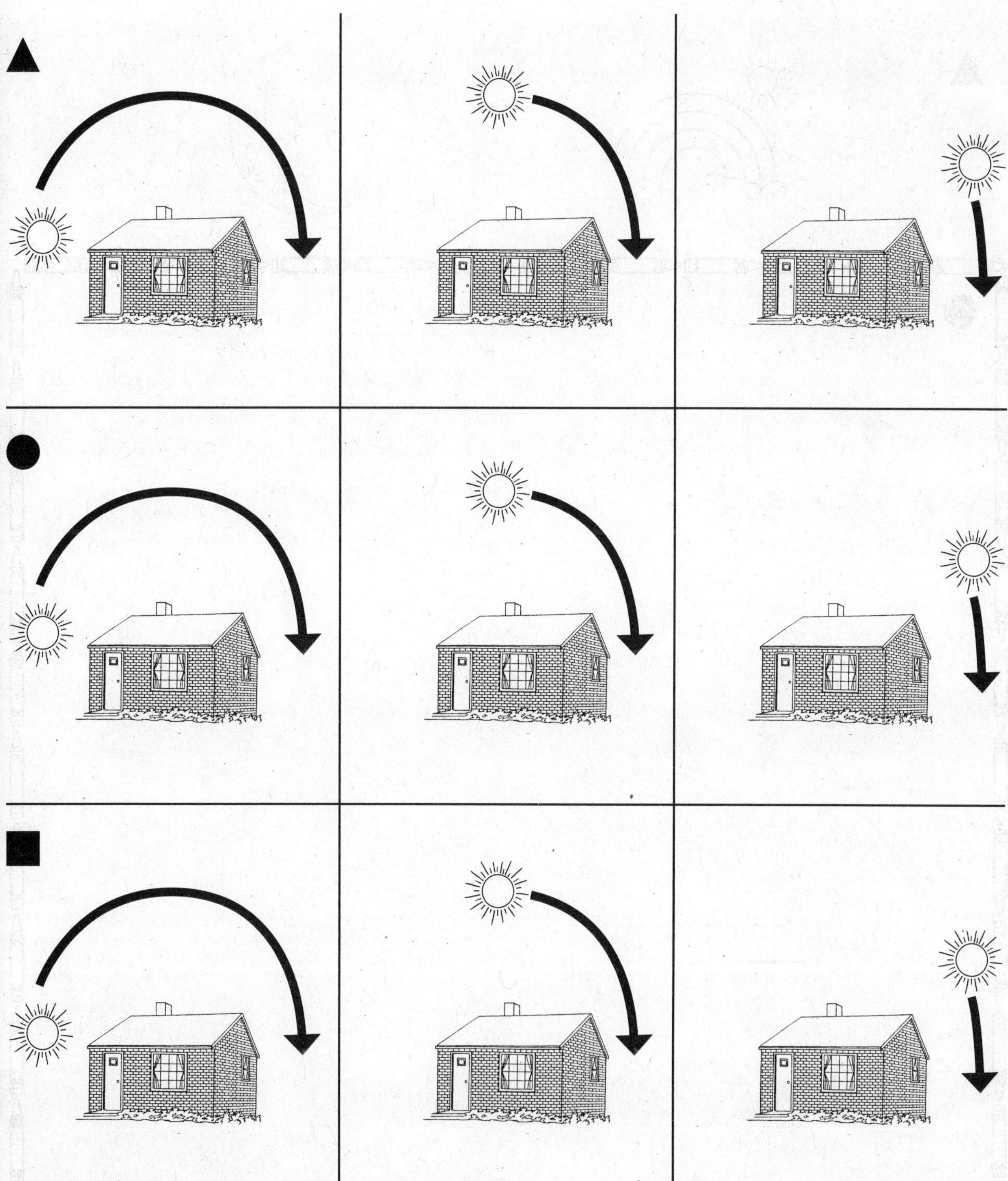

▲ Color the picture that shows a morning sun.
● Color the picture that shows a noon sun.
■ Color the picture that shows an afternoon sun.

Name ______________________

Compare

▲

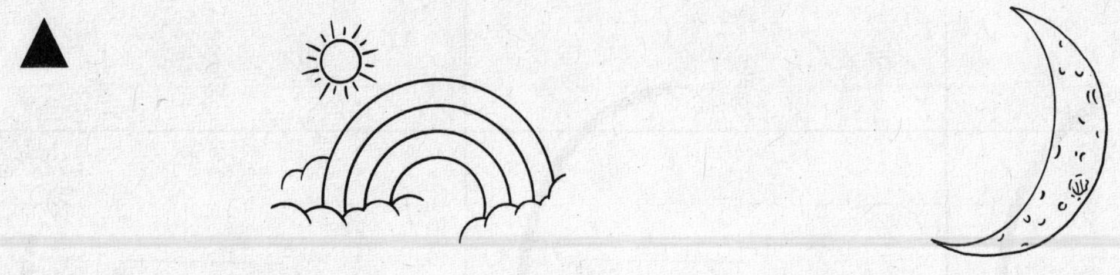

●

▲ Circle the picture of something you see at night.
● Draw a picture of something you do at nighttime.

Use with pages 77–79.

Name ___________________________

Sort

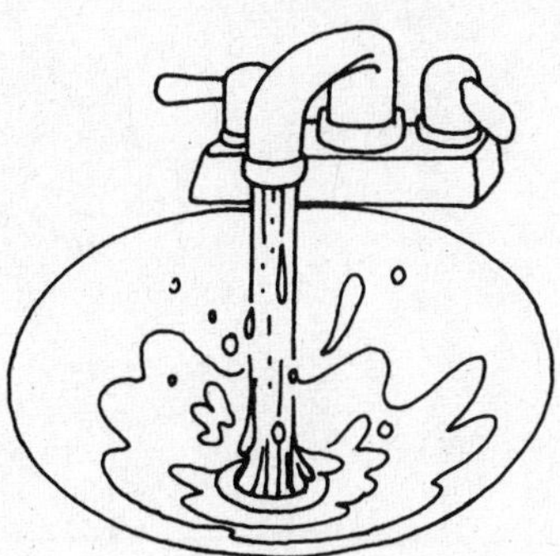

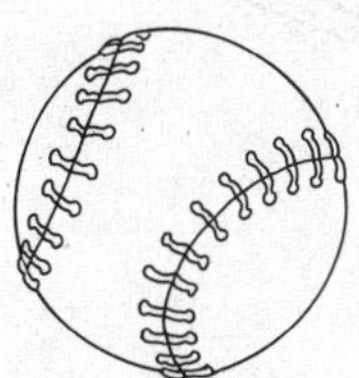

●

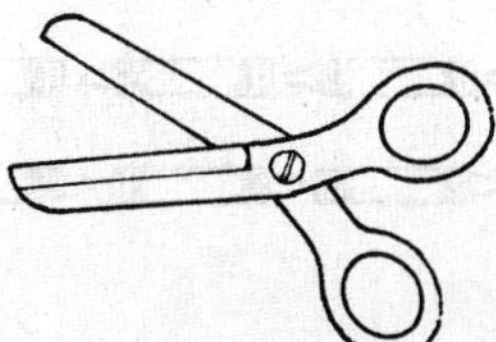

■

▲●■ Circle the pictures that show the same kind of matter.

Name ______________________

Compare

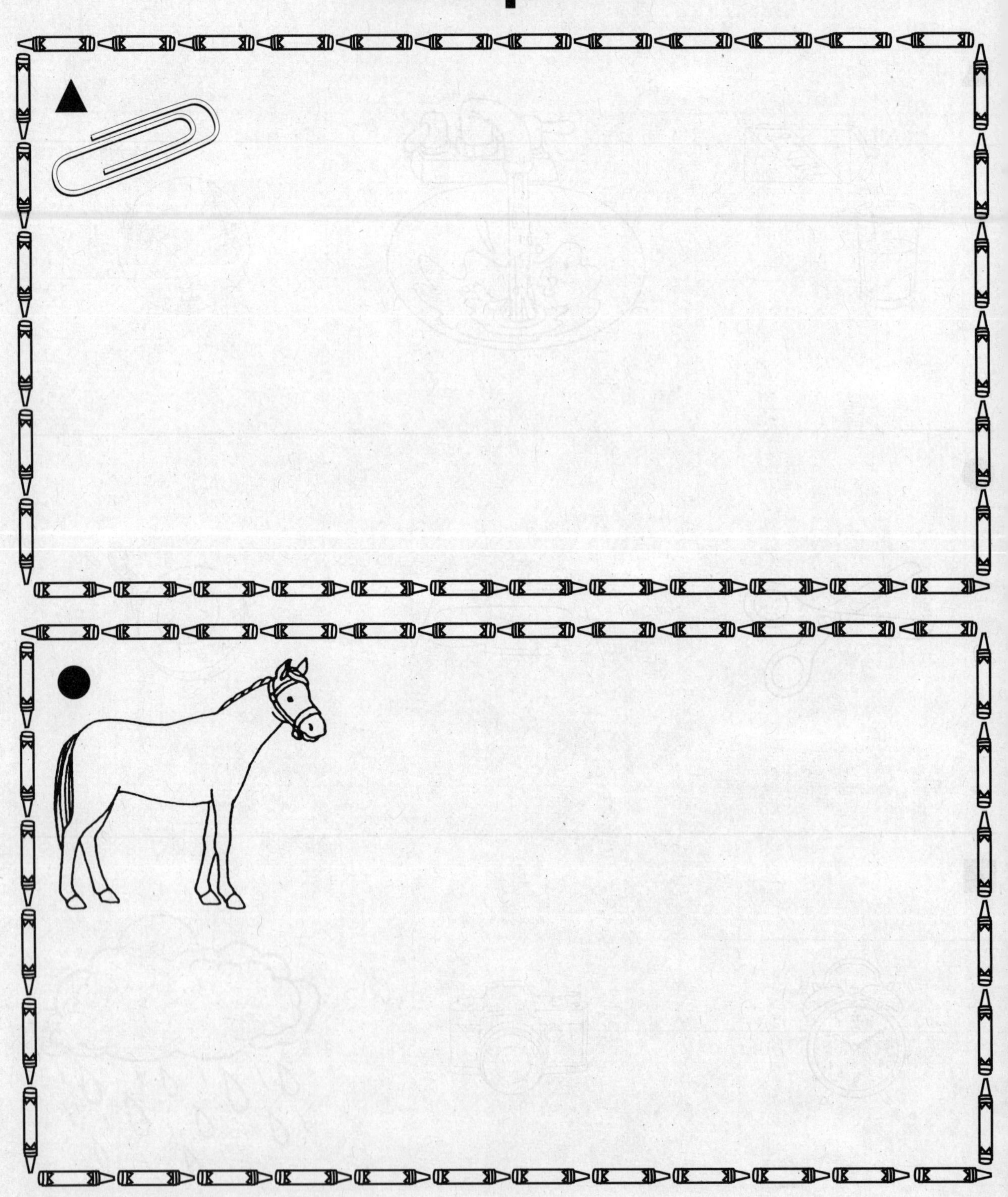

▲ Draw two other things that are small.
● Draw two other things that are big.

Use with pages 85–88.

Name ______________________________

Communicate

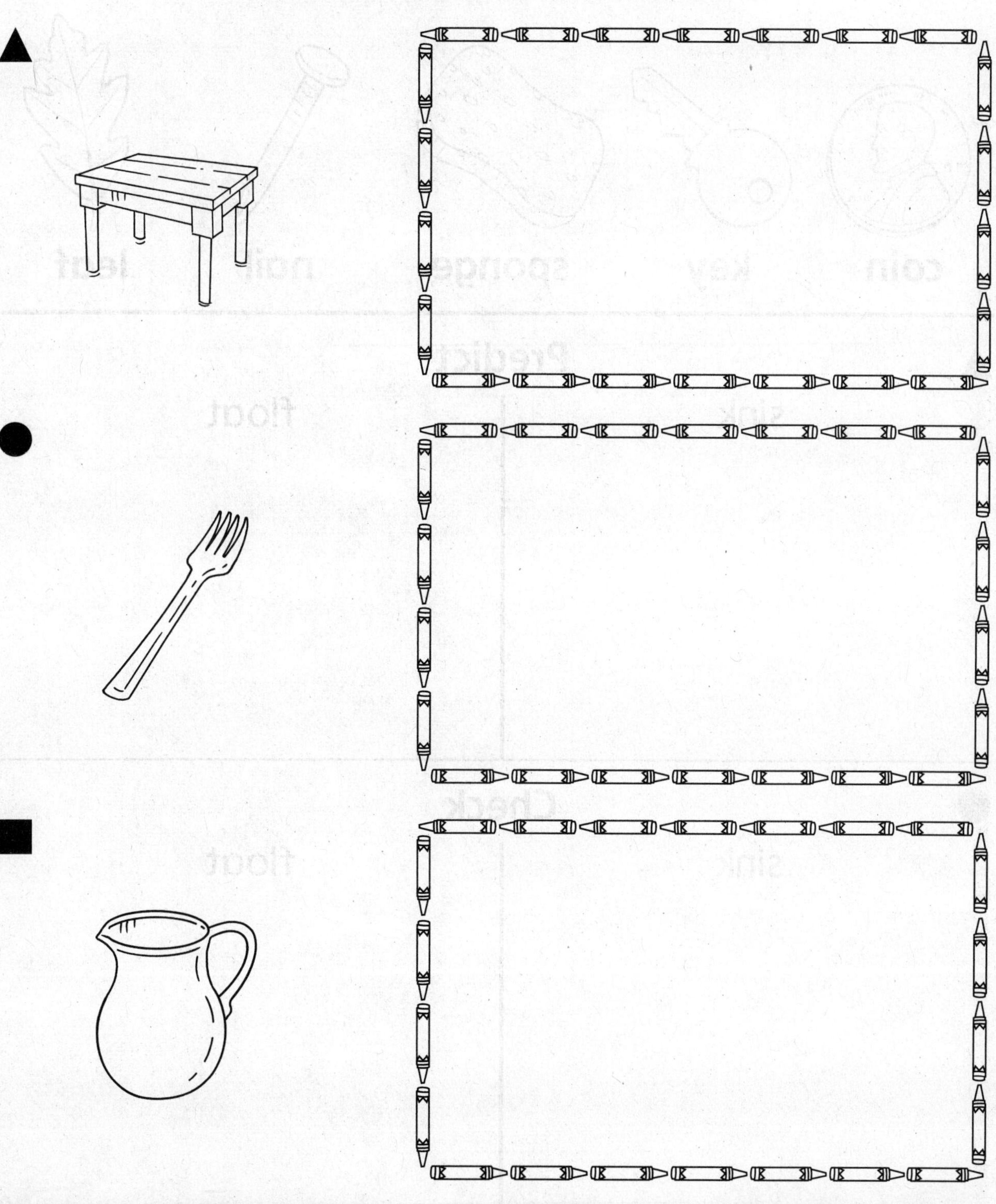

▲ A table can be made of wood. Draw another object people make from wood.
● A fork can be made of metal. Draw another object people make from metal.
■ A pitcher can be made of glass. Draw another object people make from glass.

Name ____________________

Predict

▲ **Predict**

sink	float

● **Check**

sink	float

▲ Look at the objects at the top of the page. Will the objects sink or float? Draw each object where you think it belongs.

● Check your predictions. Draw the objects where they belong. Were your predictions correct?

Name ______________________

Draw Conclusions

▲ Circle the picture that shows an object you can cut.
● Circle the picture that shows an object you can tear.
■ Circle the picture that shows an object you can fold.
★ Circle the picture that shows an object you can bend.

Use with pages 95–96.

Name ______________________________

Communicate

▲

●

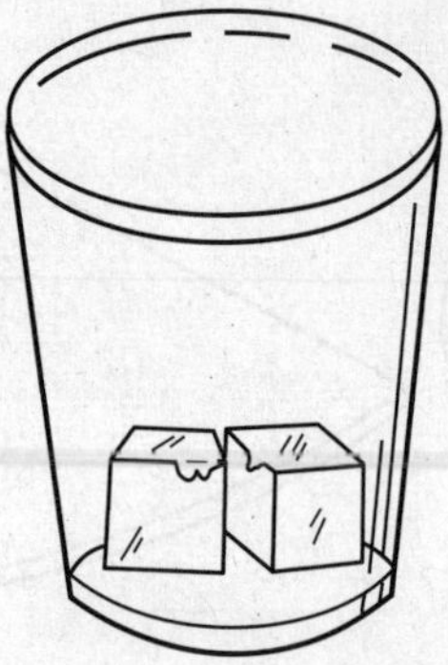

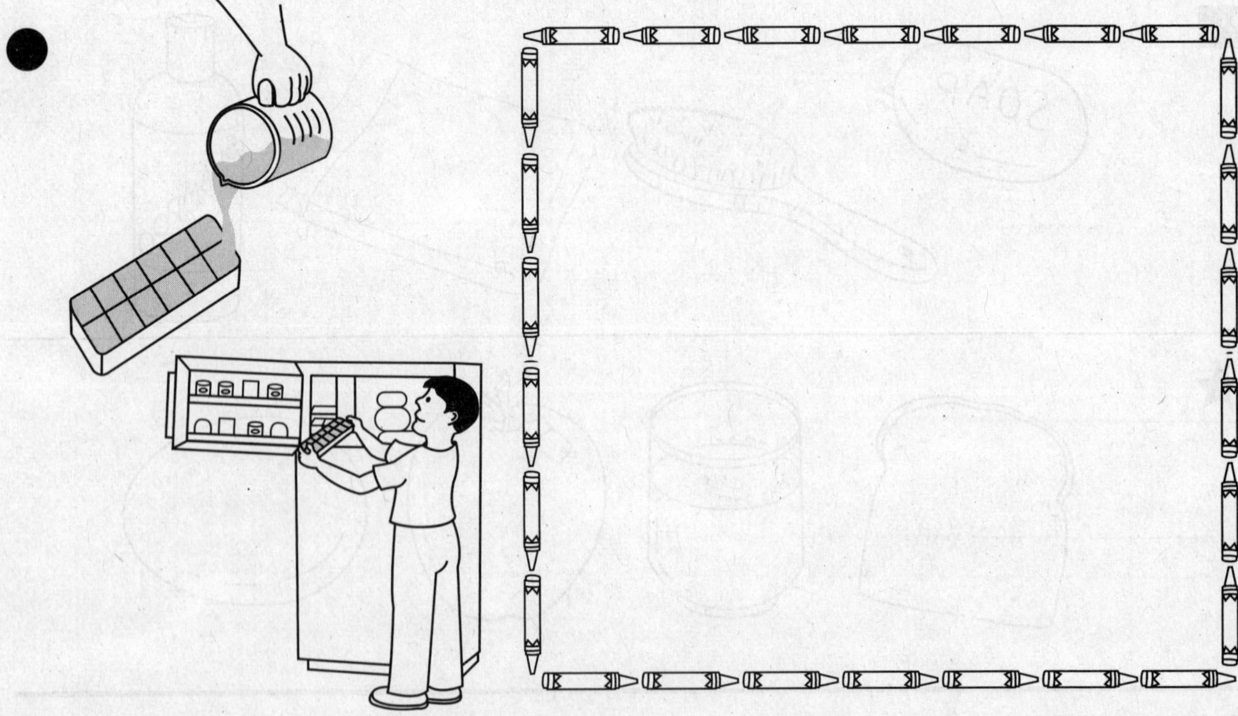

▲● Draw a picture. Show what will happen to each form of water overnight.

Use with pages 97–99.

Name ______________________________

Observe

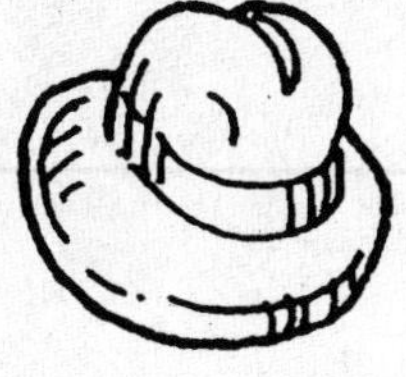

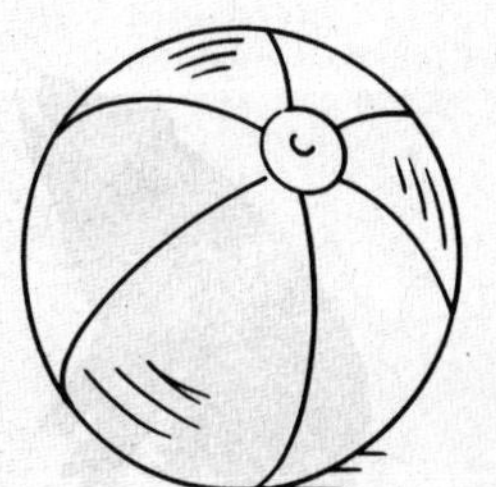

Color the pictures that show ways to protect yourself from the sun.
Mark an X on objects that don't protect you from the sun.

Name ______________________

Observe

▲

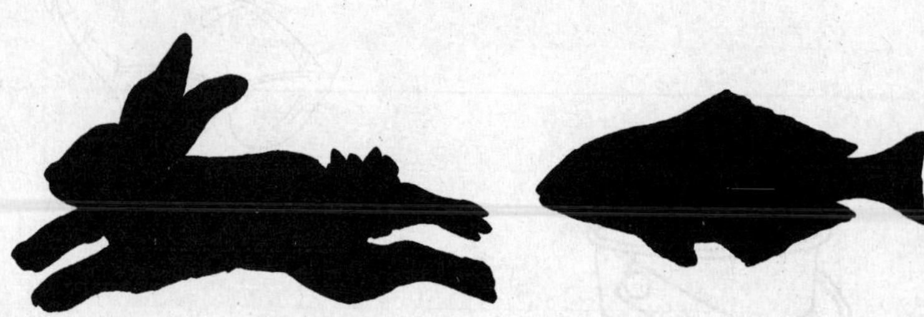

●

■

▲●■ Circle the shadow that each animal might make.

Use with pages 105–106.

Name ______________________________

Sort

Cut out the pictures. Sort them into two groups—healthful foods and foods that are not healthful. Glue each group into a sorting ring above.

Name ____________________

Make Models

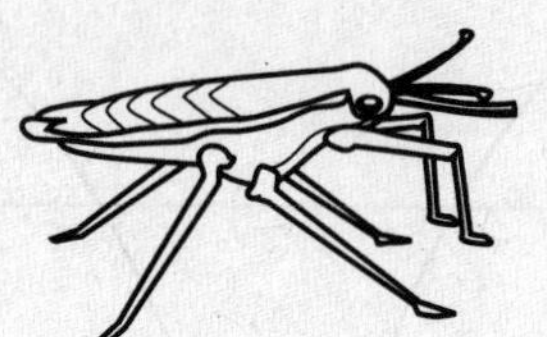

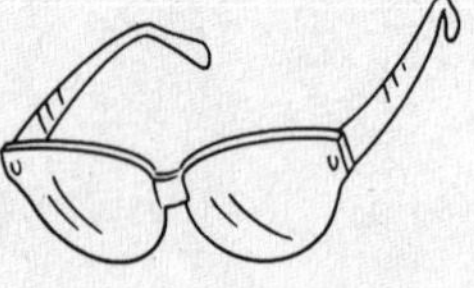
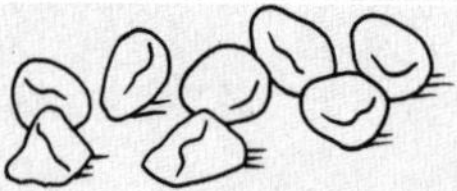

Circle the things you need to make a model of a terrarium energy system.

Use with pages 109–110.

Name ______________________________

Predict

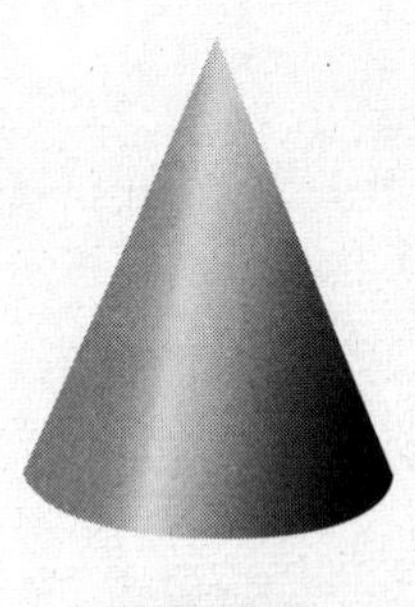

cube **sphere** **cylinder** **cone**

▲ **Predict**

yes	no

● **Check**

yes	no

▲ Look at the four solids. Which solids will roll? Draw each object where you think it belongs.

● Check your predictions. Move real solids. Draw each object where it belongs. Were your predictions correct?

Use with pages 114–116.

Name ___________________________________

Making Models

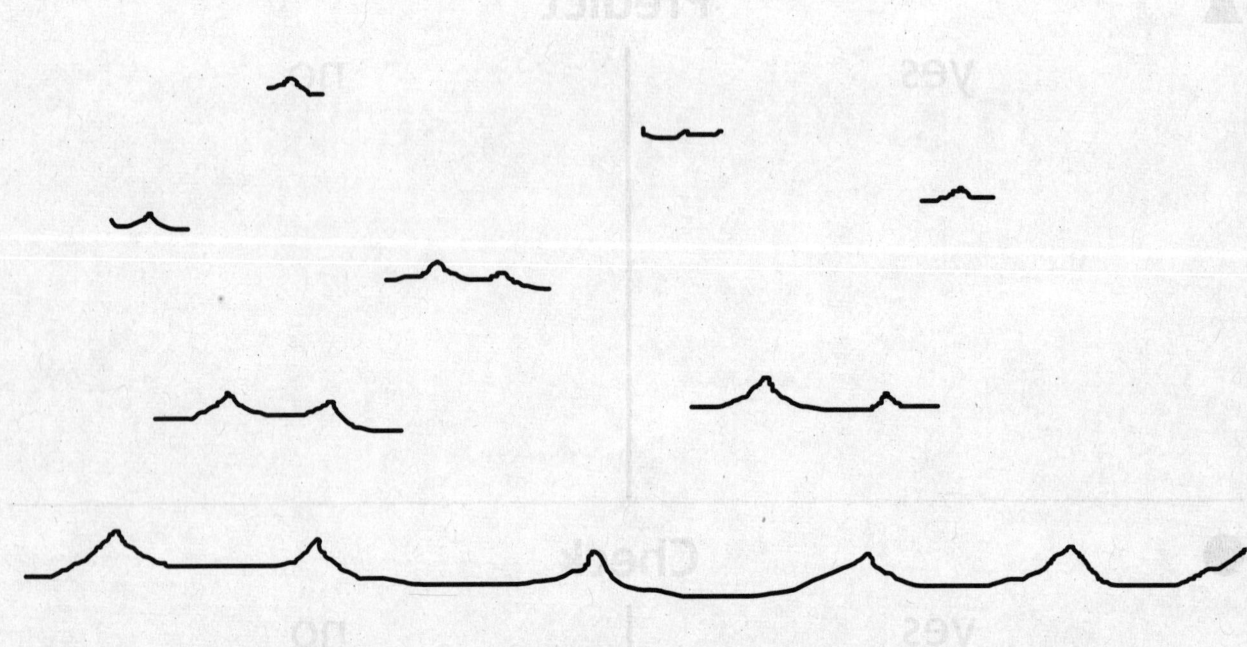

Cut out the pictures. Glue each picture in the right place to make a model of a boat.

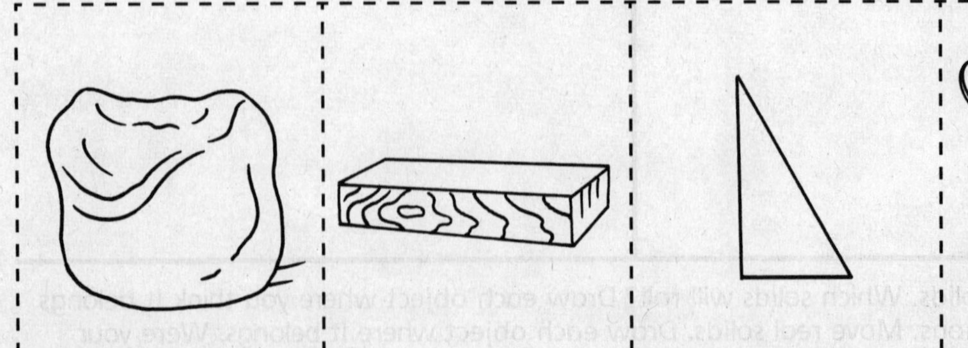

Use with pages 117–118.

Name ____________________

Predict

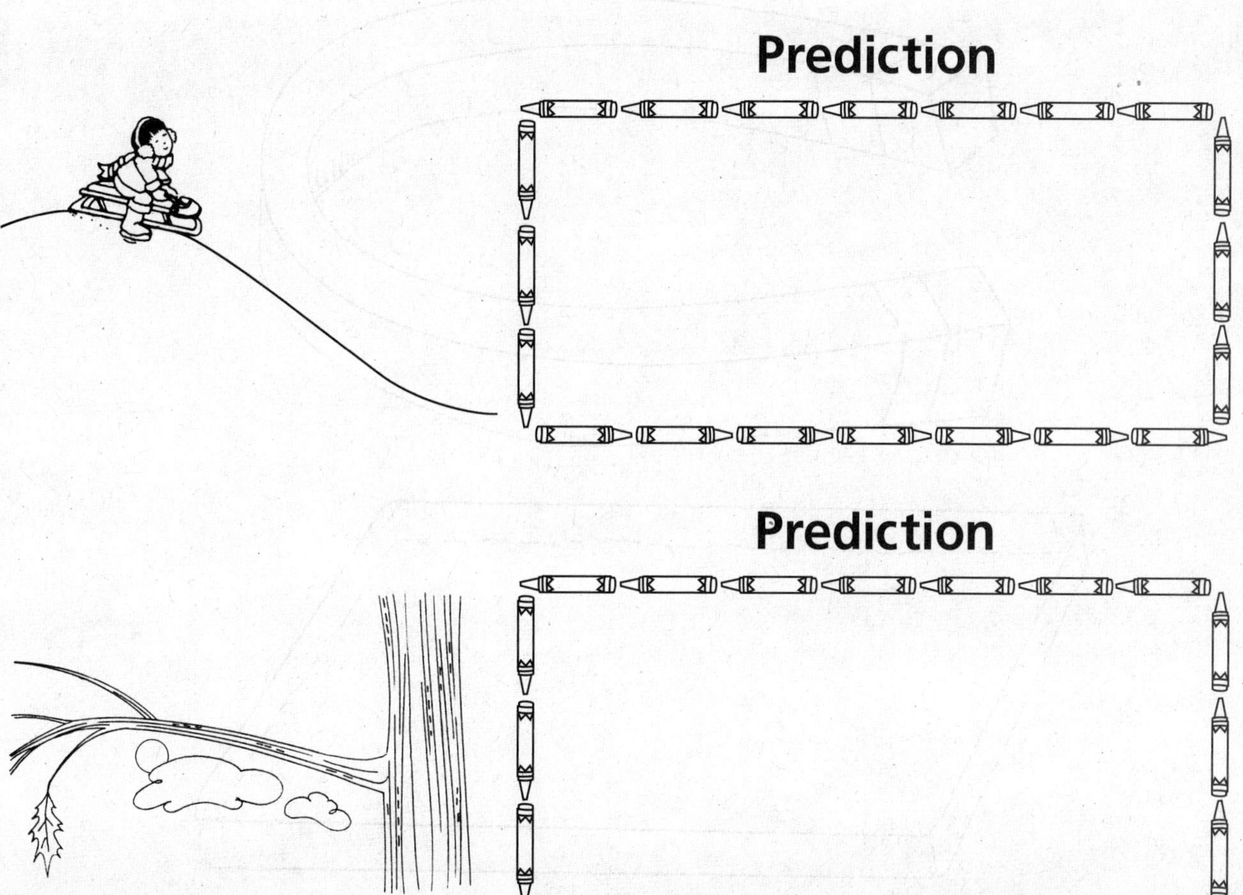

Look at the pictures. Predict what will happen to the child on the sled. Predict what will happen to the branch. In the boxes, draw what you predict will happen.

Name ______________________________

Predict

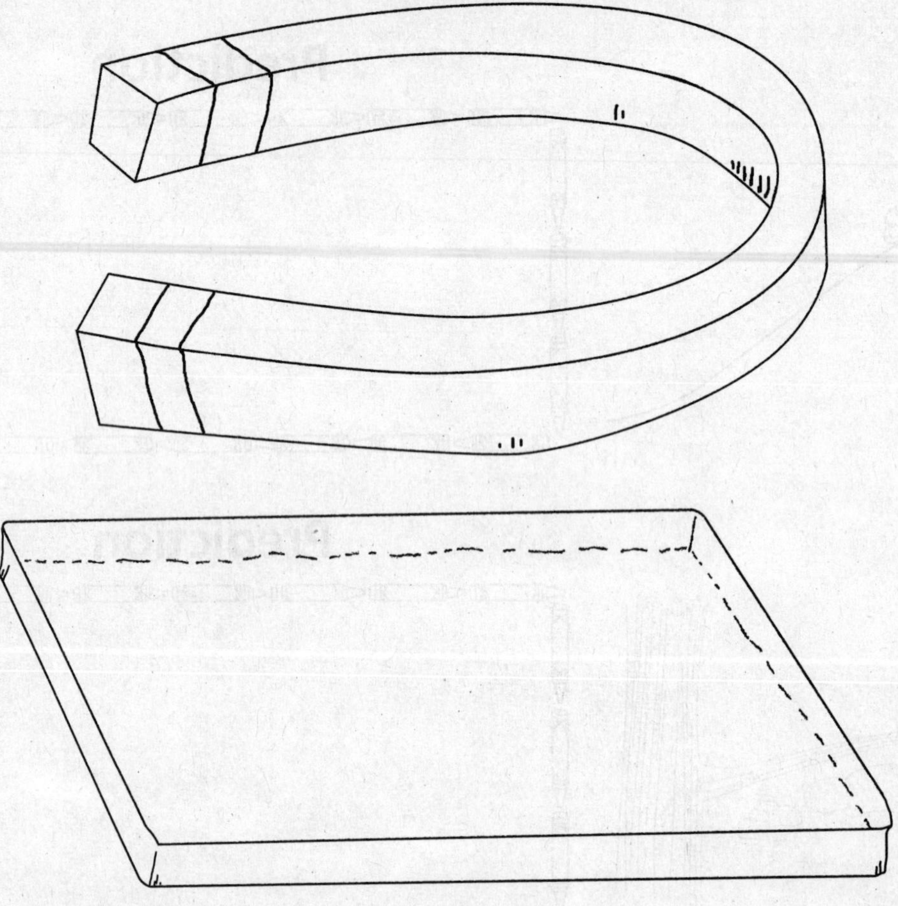

Cut out the pictures. Sort the pictures into two groups—objects a magnet attracts and objects a magnet does not attract.
Glue the objects the magnet will attract on the magnet picture.
Glue the objects the magnet will not attract on the tray picture.

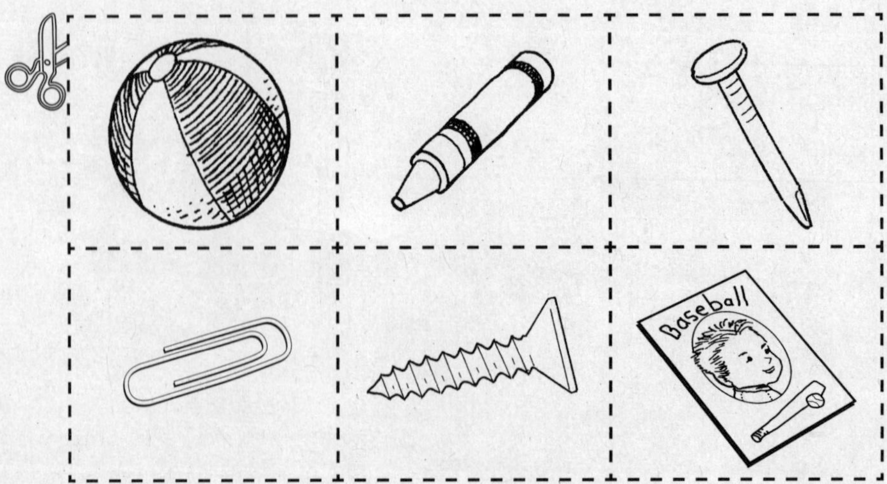

 Use with pages 123–125.

Name ______________________

Infer

Look at the objects. Which objects can a musician play? Color the objects that make music.

Name ______________________

Infer

Look at the objects. Which objects can a musician play? Color the objects that make music.

Vocabulary Card Activities

The Vocabulary Cards on pages 65–120 contain all the science vocabulary words for Kindergarten. The activities that follow suggest ways to use the word cards to

- increase children's understanding of science terms and concepts.
- help children develop their decoding skills.
- meet children's individual needs.

1 Groups

Below-Level: Give children a category of cards—for example, *senses.* Help them search through the Vocabulary Cards to find words that fit the category.

On-Level: Present children with groups of Vocabulary Cards that are clearly related in some familiar way. Give an example by modeling your thinking as you look at a set of words and consider the categories that might describe them. Have children decide what category best describes their group of cards.

Advanced: Have children work in small groups to come up with their own sets of Vocabulary Cards and categories, which they can try out on classmates.

---

2 Related or Unrelated?

Below-Level: Choose four Vocabulary Cards. Of the four, three should be related and one should be unrelated—for example, *roots, stem, leaf, animal.* Have children look at the pictures and name each one. Then have children choose the unrelated Vocabulary Card and tell why it is unrelated. Encourage children to tell why they agree or disagree. As the children become more fluent and more confident, challenge them by including two unrelated objects.

On-Level/Advanced: Have children work in groups of three or four. The group members take turns choosing four cards, three related and one unrelated. The person who chooses the cards puts them in a row. The other group members work together to determine which word is unrelated. Encourage children to discuss and defend their choices.

③ Make Up a Story

Below-Level: Choose two Vocabulary Cards that seem to go together, for example, *taste* and *touch.* Begin a story using the two words. Help children continue the story, adding Vocabulary Cards if they can.

On-Level/Advanced: Have a child choose two Vocabulary Cards that go together, put them on a desk, and use them to begin a story. Then call on a volunteer to choose another card, place it next to the first two, and continue the story. Continue to call on children to add to the story until they bring it to a logical conclusion.

---

④ Bingo

Below-Level: Have children divide a sheet of paper into a 3" × 3" grid, as in a Tic-Tac-Toe board. Give them nine letters of the alphabet to print, one per square. They should decide placement of the letters. Put various Vocabulary Cards in a bag, all starting with different letters. As a Vocabulary Card is pulled from the bag and slowly pronounced and repeated, children should determine whether the beginning sound matches the letter on their card and put a marker on that letter. As soon as a child has a row filled down, across, or diagonally, he or she should raise a hand to be declared the winner of that round.

On-Level/Advanced: Play the game as above, but let children choose their own letters to write in the squares.

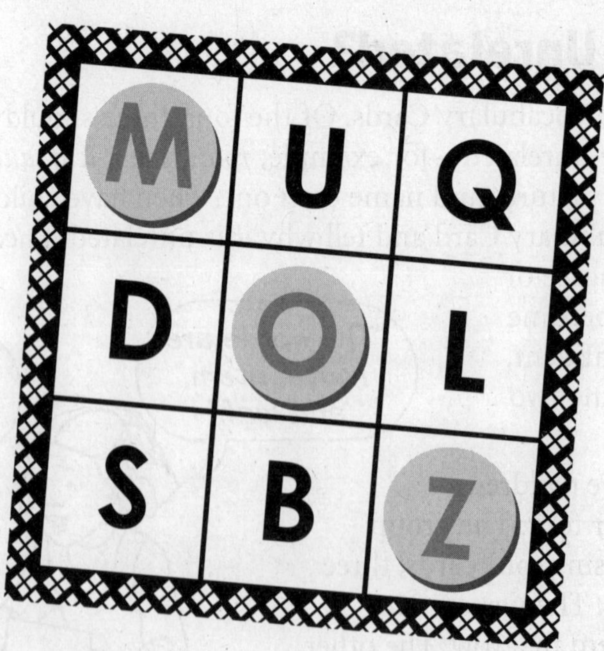

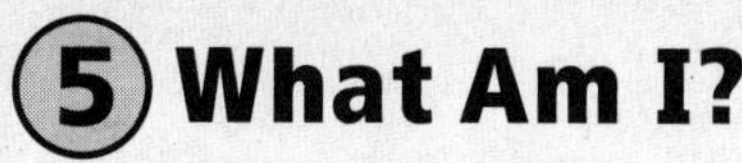

5 What Am I?

Tell children that in this game they must guess a word that is taped on their backs. Select enough words so that every child can have a different Vocabulary Card on his or her back. Be sure to choose words that are easy to describe or talk about. Explain that they will use clues given by classmates to identify the words. Tell children that their word card can be moved from back to front when they have guessed their word. Direct children to mingle, asking one another for hints about their words and giving out hints to others.

Below-Level: Model giving hints, using a volunteer with a sample word on his or her back. You may also wish to limit the number of words and have partners wear the same Vocabulary Card so they can help each other identify the word.

On-Level: You may wish to provide time prior to the activity for children to review the words and their meanings. Tell children to think about the hints they will give for each term.

Advanced: Divide the class into small groups, taping a word to each child's back. Have group members play a form of Twenty Questions. Tell each child to take a turn asking the group yes-or-no questions about the word, instead of asking for hints.

water
flower
desert
summer
wing
thermometer
insect
ocean
weather
mountain
magnet

"Am I a living thing?"
"Yes."
insect

6 Opposites Attract

Before beginning the activity, separate pairs of opposites from the Vocabulary Cards. Choose six other word cards that can be used as distracters. To begin, discuss what opposite means, using common opposites such as *up* and *down*, *hard* and *easy*, *tall* and *short*, *day* and *night*.

Below-Level: Display pairs of opposites. Discuss how the two words in each set differ in meaning. Then have children choose a pair to illustrate, showing graphically how the words are opposite in meaning. Ask children to share their drawings.

On-Level/Advanced: Present one Vocabulary Card to children and talk about the word's meaning. Have children find a word in the deck that has an opposite meaning. Discuss how these two words differ in meaning.

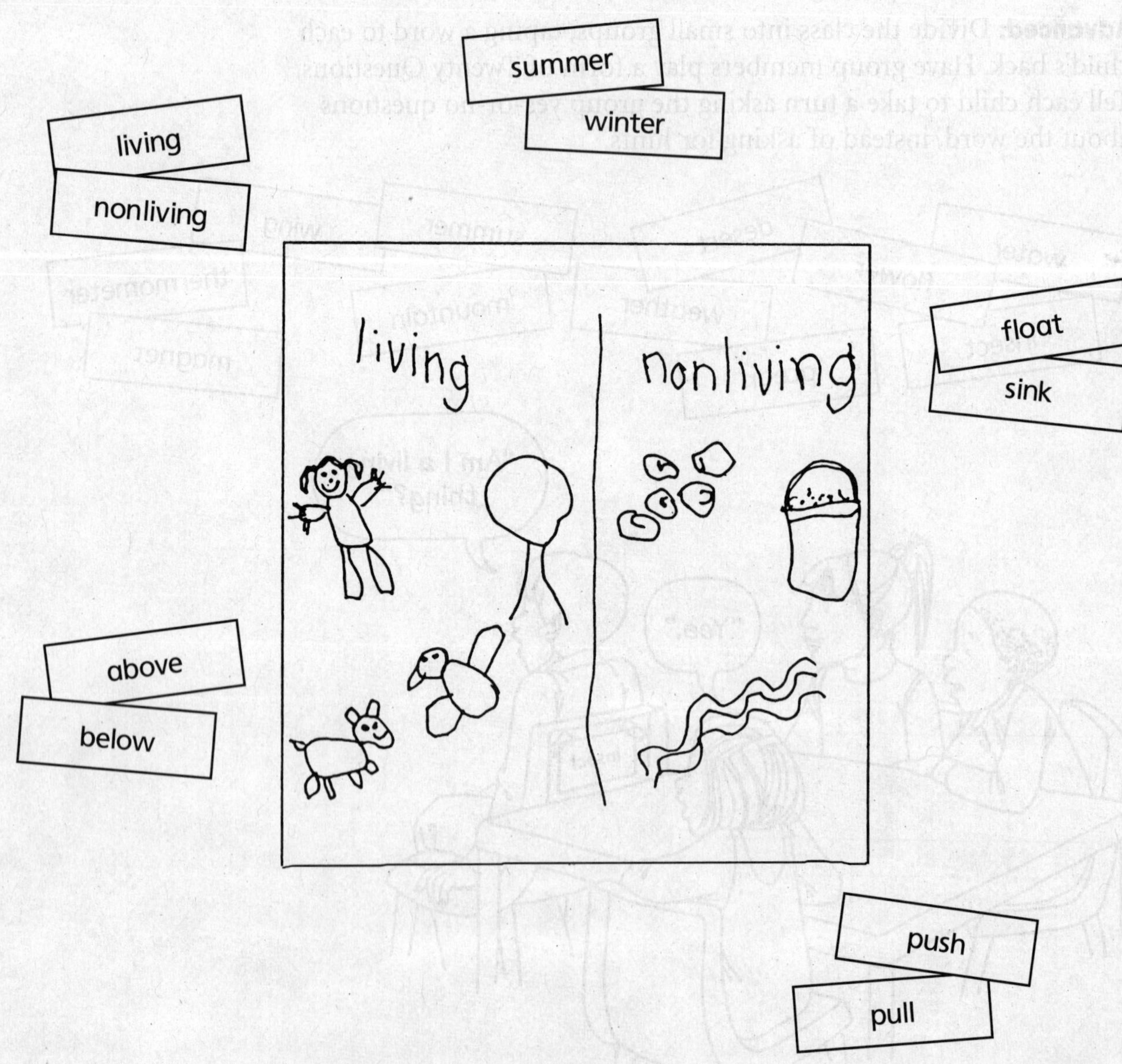

1

above

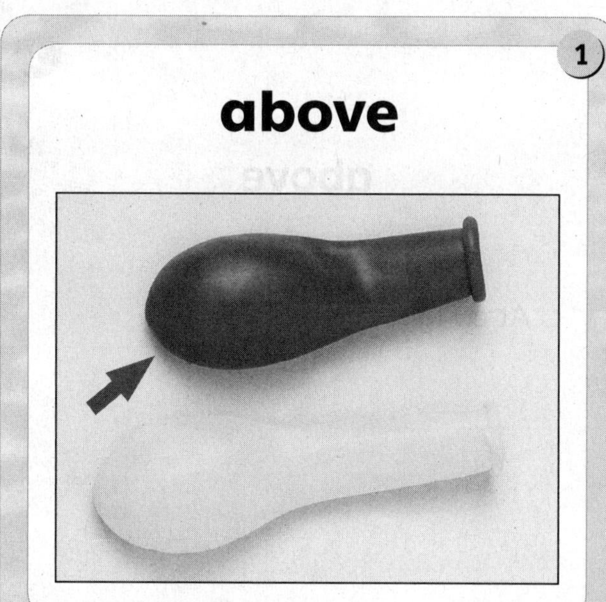

2

air

3

animal

4

arm

2

air

Something that people and land animals breathe to live.

1

above

At a higher place.

4

arm

A part of an animal's body. The arm connects the shoulder and the hand.

3

animal

A living thing that can not make its own food.

5

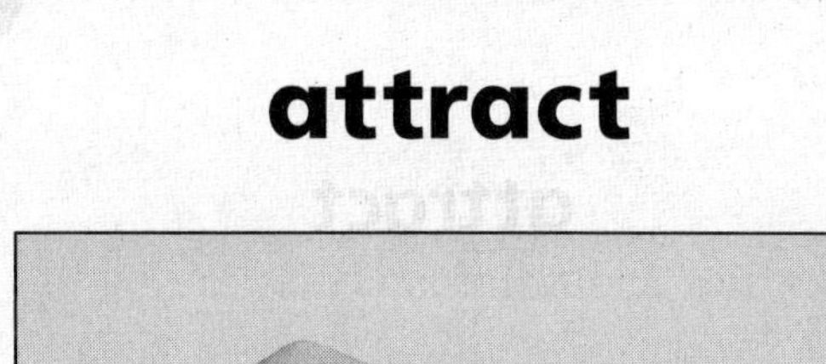

attract

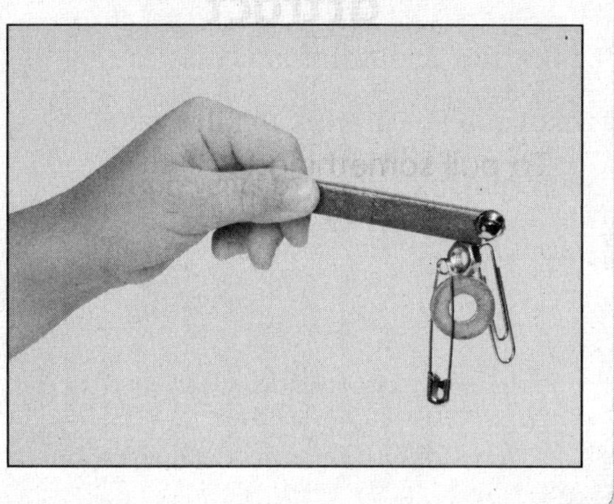

6

balance

7

below

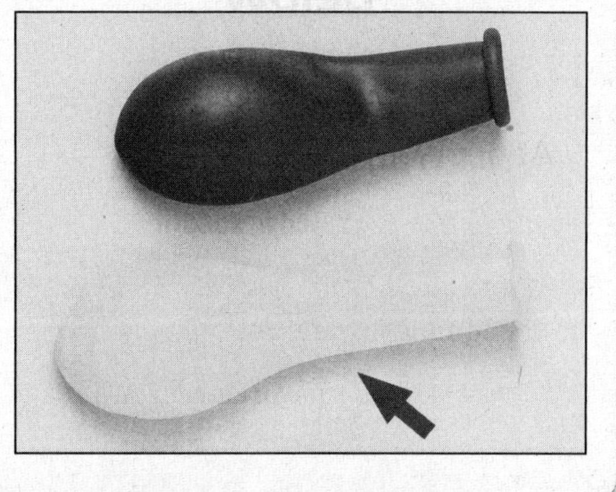

8

bird

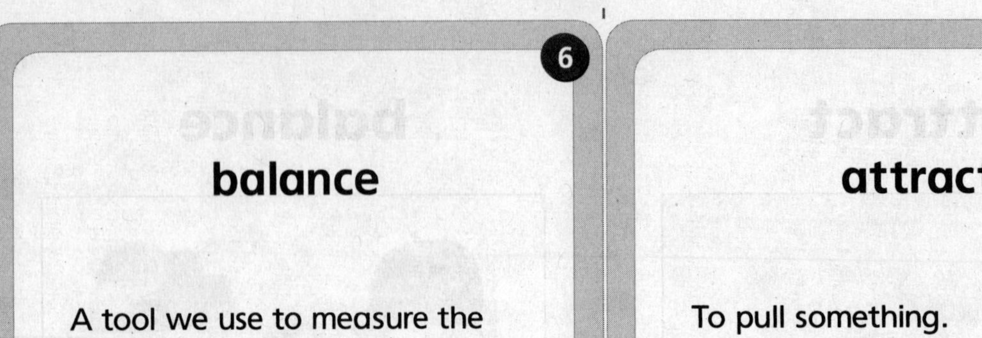

6

balance

A tool we use to measure the mass of an object.

5

attract

To pull something.

8

bird

The only kind of animal that has feathers.

7

below

At a lower place.

9

calves

10

chicks

11

color

12

conserve

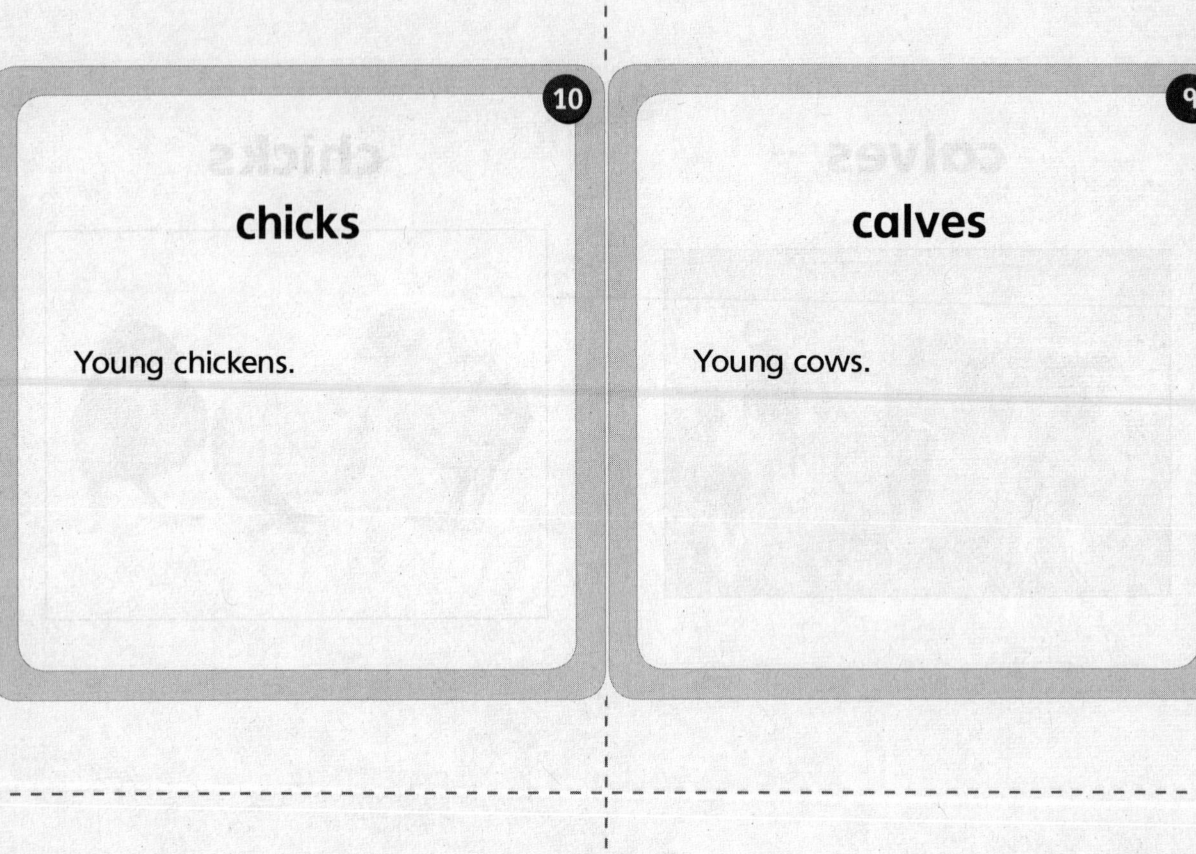

10

chicks

Young chickens.

9

calves

Young cows.

12

conserve

To use something carefully so that it will last and not be used up.

11

color

A physical property of an object that you can see. Red, blue, and yellow are colors.

13

cubs

14

curved

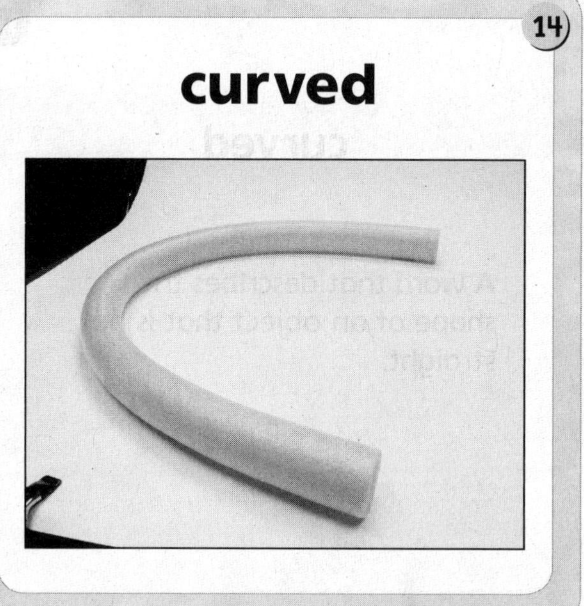

15

describe

16

different

14

curved

A word that describes the shape of an object that is not straight.

13

cubs

The young of some animals such as bears.

16

different

Not the same as something else.

15

describe

To tell about something.

17

energy

18

evaporation

19

fall

20

feathers

18

evaporation

The moving of water into the air. The liquid water becomes a gas that we can not see.

17

energy

Something that can cause change. Most energy on Earth comes from the sun. People, animals, and plants get energy from food.

20

feathers

The kind of body covering a bird has.

19

fall

The season that comes after summer, when the weather gets cooler and drier.

21

fish

22

float

23

flower

24

food

22

float

To stay on top of a liquid.

21

fish

A kind of animal that is covered in scales, uses gills to take in oxygen, and lives in water.

24

food

Something that people and animals eat to live and grow. Plants make their own food.

23

flower

The plant part that makes seeds that can become new plants.

25

force

26

fur

27

gas

28

grass

26

fur

The kind of body covering a bear or a cat has.

25

force

A push or a pull that can make an object move.

28

grass

A kind of plant with long, thin leaves.

27

gas

A kind of matter that does not have its own shape. It fills all of its container.

29

gravity

30

grow

31

habitat

32

hand lens

30

grow

To change and get bigger.

29

gravity

A force that pulls things toward the center of Earth.

32

hand lens

A tool we use to help us see small things. It makes them look bigger.

31

habitat

A place where a living thing has the food, water, and shelter it needs to live.

33

hearing

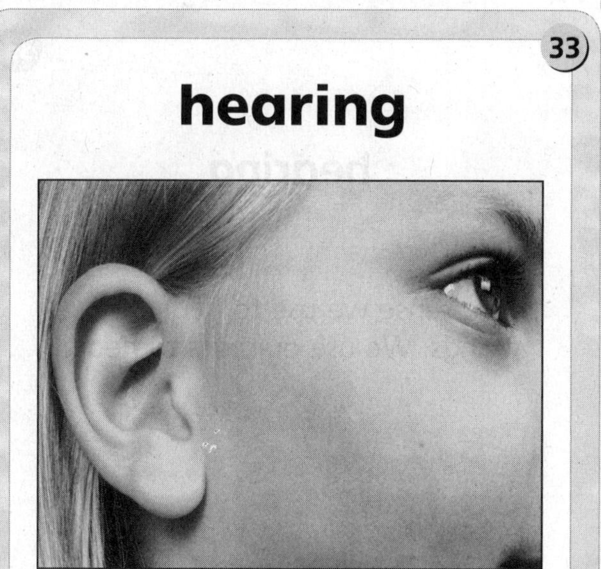

34

heat

35

insect

36

investigate

34

heat

Energy that warms.

33

hearing

The sense we use to hear things. We use our ears to hear.

36

investigate

To plan and do a test.

35

insect

A kind of animal that has three body parts and six legs.

37

land

38

leaf

39

left

40

leg

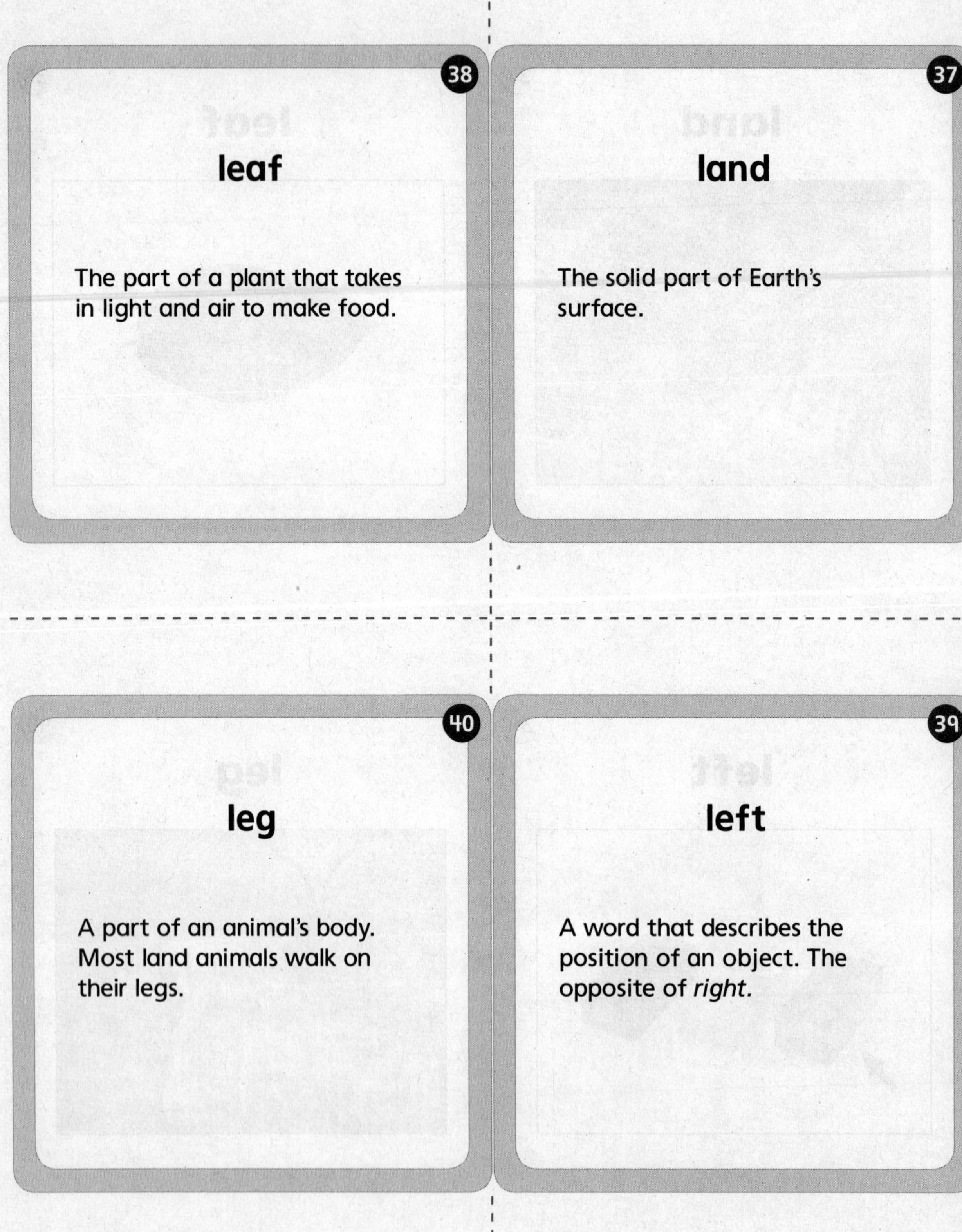

38

leaf

The part of a plant that takes in light and air to make food.

37

land

The solid part of Earth's surface.

40

leg

A part of an animal's body. Most land animals walk on their legs.

39

left

A word that describes the position of an object. The opposite of *right*.

41

life cycle

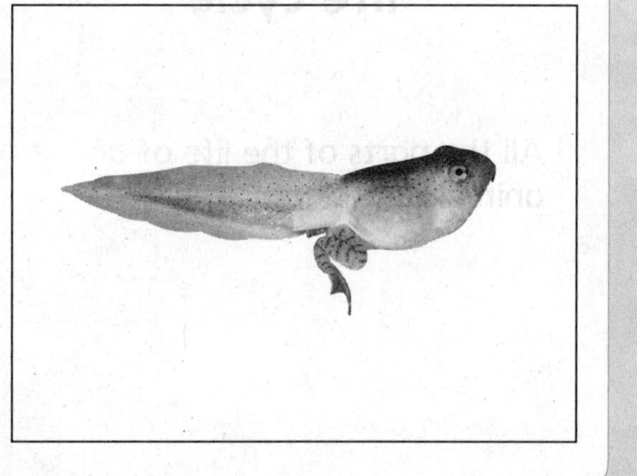

42

light

43

liquid

44

living

42

light

Energy that lets us see things.

41

life cycle

All the parts of the life of an animal or a plant.

44

living

Needing food, water, and air to grow and change.

43

liquid

A kind of matter that flows and takes the shape of its container.

45

magnet

46

matter

47

mix

48

moon

46

matter

The material all things are made of.

45

magnet

An object that attracts things made of iron and steel.

48

moon

A huge ball of rock in the sky that does not give off its own light.

47

mix

To put together.

49

natural resource

50

nonliving

51

observe

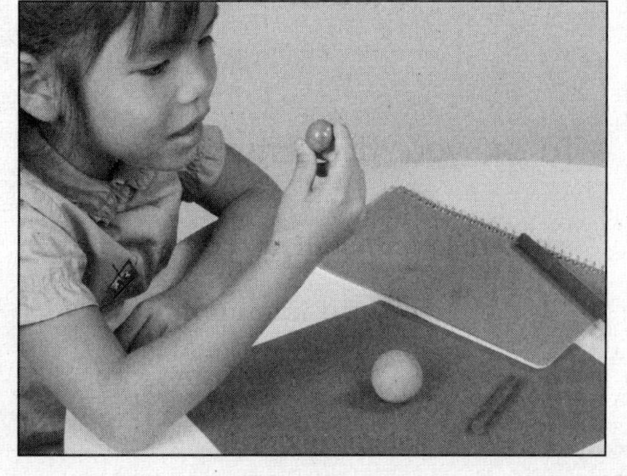

52

ocean

50

nonliving

Not needing food, water, and air and not growing.

49

natural resource

Anything from nature that people can use.

52

ocean

A large body of salty water.

51

observe

To use your five senses to learn.

53

over

54

planet

55

plant

56

pull

54

planet

A large body that orbits the sun.

53

over

A word that describes an object that is above another object.

56

pull

To move something toward oneself.

55

plant

A living thing that makes its own food.

57

push

58

question

59

rain

60

rain gauge

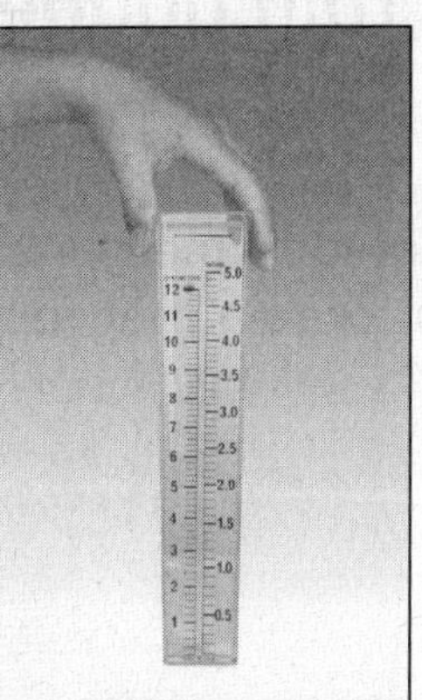

58

question

A sentence that asks about something.

57

push

To move something away from oneself.

60

rain gauge

A tool used to measure the amount of rain that falls.

59

rain

Drops of fresh water that fall from clouds.

61

recycle

62

reuse

63

right

64

river

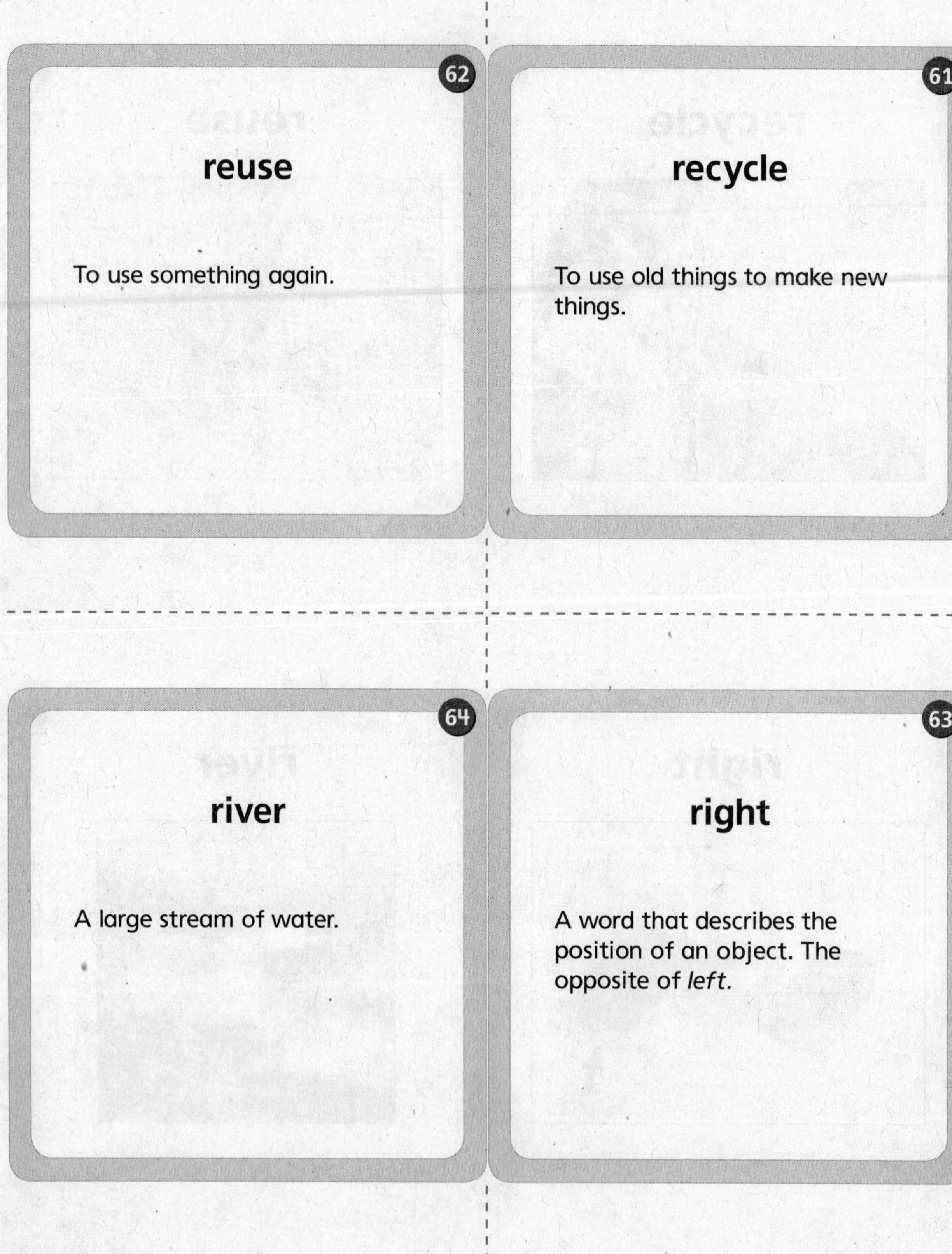

62

reuse

To use something again.

61

recycle

To use old things to make new things.

64

river

A large stream of water.

63

right

A word that describes the position of an object. The opposite of *left*.

65

rock

66

roots

67

rough

68

sand

66

roots

The parts of a plant that hold it in the soil and take in water and other nutrients.

65

rock

A hard, nonliving thing that comes from Earth.

68

sand

Tiny grains of rock worn away from large rocks.

67

rough

A word that describes how an object feels when it is not smooth.

69

scales

70

season

71

seed

72

senses

70

season

A time of year. A year has four seasons.

69

scales

The kind of body covering a fish or snake has.

72

senses

The ways parts of our bodies tell us what the world is like. The five senses are sight, hearing, smell, taste, and touch.

71

seed

The part of many plants from which a new plant grows.

73

shade

74

shadow

75

shape

76

shelter

74

shadow

A dark shape formed when light is blocked by an object.

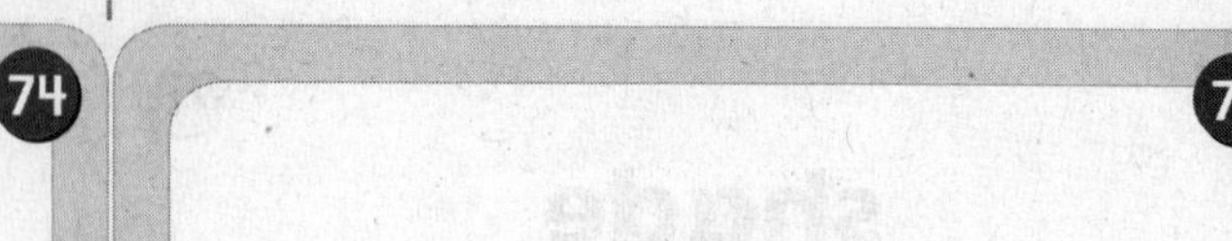

73

shade

An outside area with less light where the sun has been blocked by a cloud or a large object, such as a house.

76

shelter

A place where a living thing can be safe.

75

shape

The form of an object.

77

shrub

78

sight

79

similar

80

sink

78

sight

The sense we use to see things. We see with our eyes.

77

shrub

A kind of plant with many small woody stems. It is also called a bush.

80

sink

To fall to the bottom of a liquid.

79

similar

The same in some ways but not exactly the same.

81

size

82

skin

83

smell

84

smooth

82

skin

The kind of body covering a frog or a salamander has. People also have skin. Animals such as cats have skin under their fur. Birds have skin under their feathers.

81

size

The amount of space an object takes up.

84

smooth

A word that describes how an object feels when it is not bumpy.

83

smell

The sense we use to smell things. We smell with our noses.

85

snow

86

soil

87

solid

88

sound

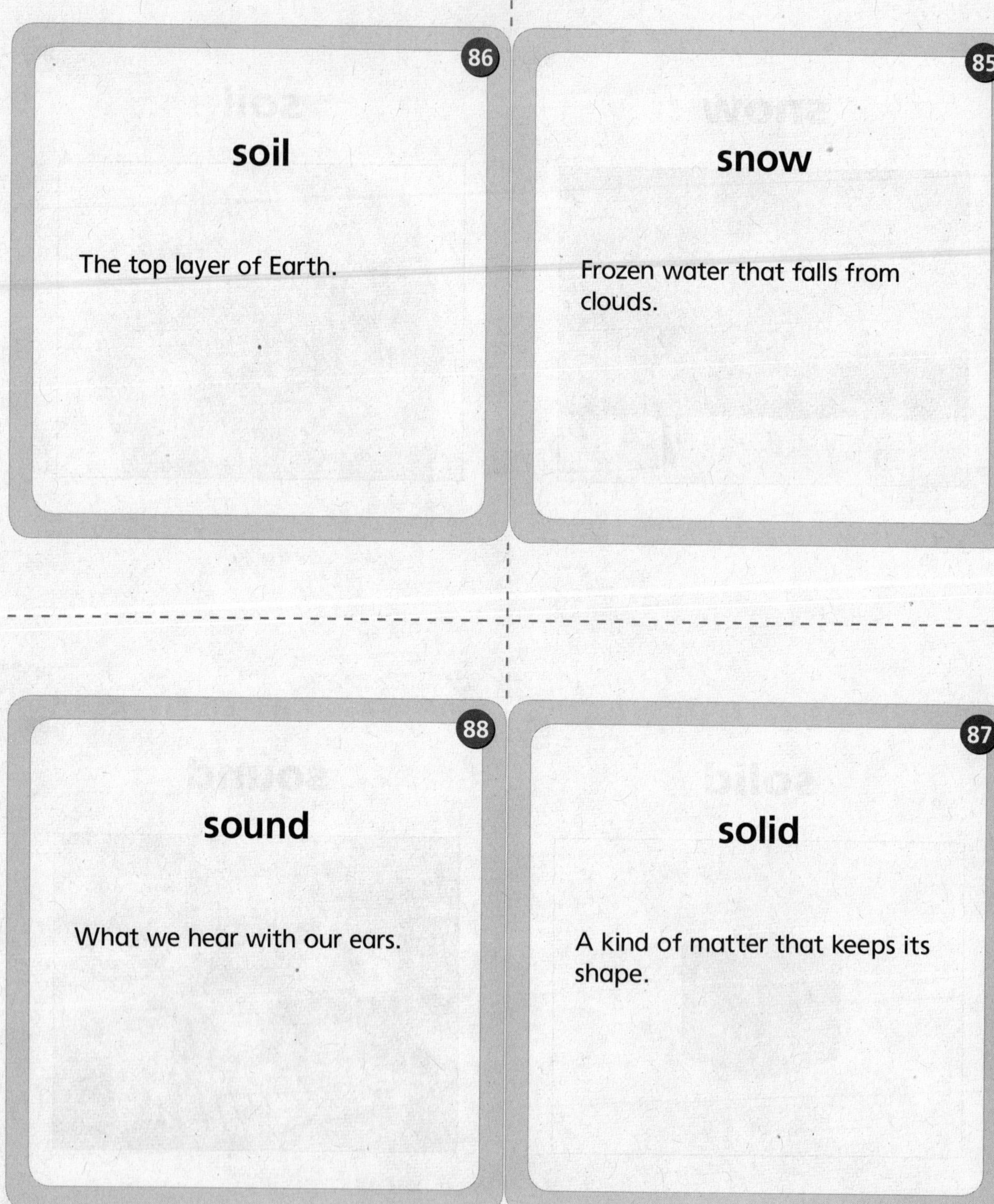

86

soil

The top layer of Earth.

85

snow

Frozen water that falls from clouds.

88

sound

What we hear with our ears.

87

solid

A kind of matter that keeps its shape.

89

speed

90

spring

91

star

92

stem

90

spring

The season after winter, when the weather gets warmer and wetter.

89

speed

The measure of how fast something moves.

92

stem

The plant part that holds up a plant. It carries food and water through a plant.

91

star

An object in the sky that gives off its own light.

93

summer

94

sun

95

sunlight

96

taste

94

sun

A star that gives heat and light to Earth.

93

summer

The season with warm weather and the longest days.

96

taste

The sense we use to taste things. We taste with our mouths.

95

sunlight

Light that comes from the sun.

97

temperature

98

terrarium

99

texture

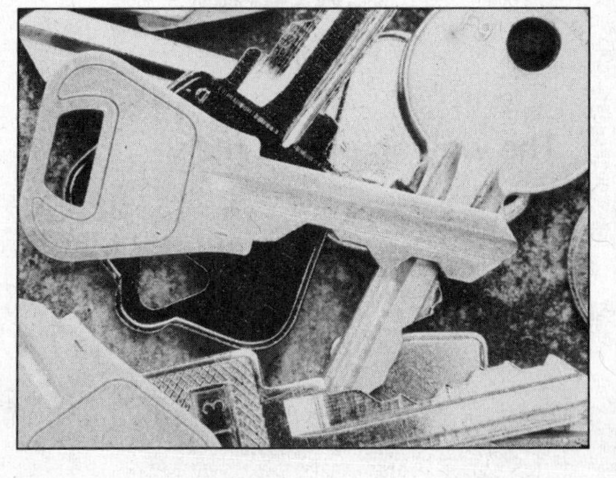

100

thermometer

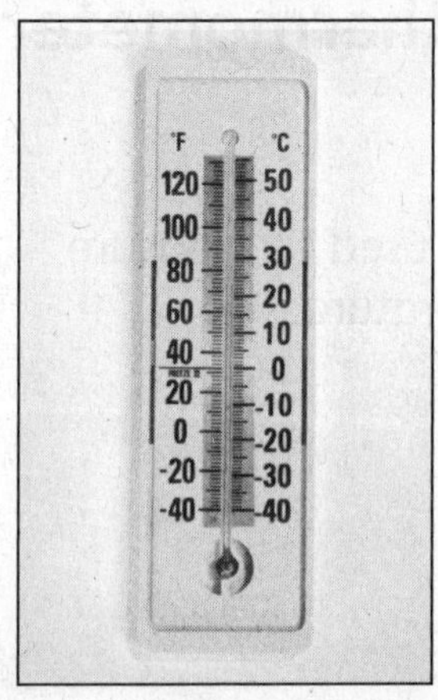

98

terrarium

A container in which plants and animals live on soil.

97

temperature

The measure of how hot or cold something is.

100

thermometer

A tool used to measure temperature.

99

texture

The way an object feels.

101

tool

102

touch

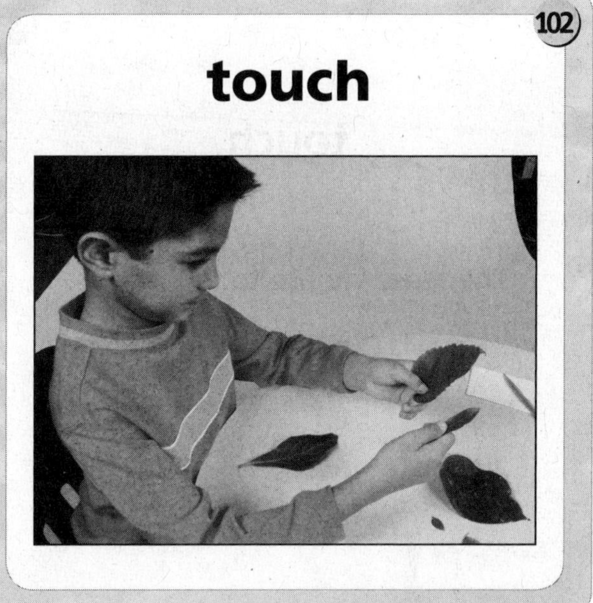

103

tree

104

under

102

touch

The sense we use to feel things.

101

tool

Something we can use to help us find out about things.

104

under

A word that describes an object that is below something.

103

tree

A kind of plant with a woody stem called a trunk and woody branches.

105

vibration

106

water

107

weather

108

weight

106

water

A clear liquid found in Earth's lakes, rivers, and oceans.

105

vibration

Movement back and forth.

108

weight

How heavy something is.

107

weather

What the air outside is like.

109

wind

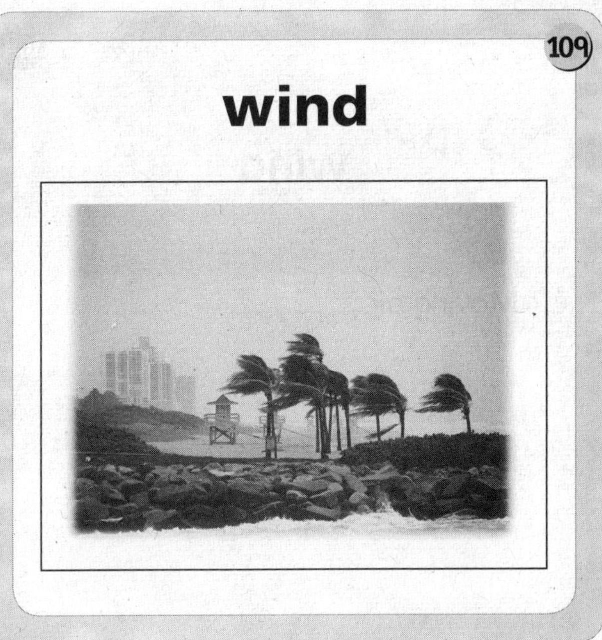

110

wind vane

111

wing

112

winter

110

wind vane

A tool used to find out the direction of the wind.

109

wind

Moving air.

112

winter

The season with cold weather and the shortest days.

111

wing

A part of an animal's body. Wings help many birds and insects fly. Bats also have wings.